A CAPITAL CAPITAL CITY

1790–1814

Suzanne Hilton

Atheneum ★ 1992 ★ New York
Maxwell Macmillan Canada • *Toronto*
Maxwell Macmillan International
New York • Oxford • Singapore • Sydney

The author wishes to thank Kathryn S. Smith of the Historical Society of Washington, D.C., for her careful reading of the manuscript.

Atheneum
Macmillan Publishing Company
866 Third Avenue
New York, NY 10022

Maxwell Macmillan Canada, Inc.
1200 Eglinton Avenue East
Suite 200
Don Mills, Ontario M3C 3N1

Macmillan Publishing Company is part of the Maxwell Communication Group of Companies.

First edition

Printed in the United States of America

10 9 8 7 6 5 4 3 2 1

The text of this book is set in Old Style Number 7.

Designed by Kathryn Parise

Library of Congress Cataloging-in-Publication Data

Hilton, Suzanne.
A capital capital city, 1790–1814 / by Suzanne Hilton
p.   cm.
Includes bibliographical references and index.
Summary: Provides a look at the planning, people, and process involved in the establishment of Washington, D.C., and describes the first twenty-five years of its growth.
ISBN 0–689–31641–0
1. Washington (D.C.)—History—Juvenile literature. [1. Washington (D.C.)—History.
2. United States—History—1783–1815.] I. Title.
F197.H64   1992   91–31340
975.3′02—dc20

Contents

Contents

A Capital City on Paper

"Not a river in America is capable of being rendered more secure of an attack by water than the Potowmack."
—Tobias Lear in 1793

One day in 1793, President George Washington handed a special job to Tobias Lear, his secretary. Lear was to write a pamphlet about a city that did not yet exist. Worse yet, most Americans did not even want the city.

Citizens from the north said the capital city of the new United States ought to be in New York or Philadelphia. Those were modern cities that were already built. They had good, hard dirt roads, wharfs where oceangoing ships could unload cargo, and markets where people went every day to buy their food. Both cities had rivers to supply plenty of drinking water, and both had already designed a large palace for the president to live in, as soon as the men in Congress chose which one was to become the capital city.

Southerners said Charleston in South Carolina was the best place for the country's capital city. That city had a

1

harbor right on the sea. Almost every day someone told George Washington about another city that should be the nation's capital.

But Washington could be very stubborn about something he believed in deeply. He said the capital city had to be near the center of the states, if only to make it easier for the congressmen to travel to and from their homes. He also knew that the Potomac River began farther inland toward the west than any other river on the East Coast. Someday, after a series of canals had been built, the new capital could become a great center of commerce.

George Washington already knew the perfect place. He had camped overnight there when he was seventeen, on his way to do a survey of another man's land. He remembered it on a frosty night, when the sky was filled with more stars than he had ever seen at one time. Toward the east was a branch of the Potomac River, a deep basin where large ships might lie protected from storms. Stretching southward, like a silver satin ribbon, the Potomac River flowed gently down past Mount Vernon, into Chesapeake Bay and out to sea.

A few years after that, Washington had surveyed and laid out the city of Alexandria in Virginia. Then the small village of Georgetown began to grow across the river in Maryland. Both towns were almost—but not quite—where he wanted to build his capital city.

Now, forty years later, Washington had the chance to build the city he had dreamed of. But he needed some way to tell people more about his dream city. That was why Lear had to write his book, to tell people all the small details they might want to learn about it.

In 1790 the first Congress established a federal district on sixty-three square miles of land ceded by Maryland and thirty-seven given by Virginia. Later they made the district

SUTER'S TAVERN (1791)

Suter's Tavern in Georgetown, later called the Fountain Inn, was the nearest place to find a room and meal when the federal city began growing in 1791. (*The National Archives*)

larger by including the town of Alexandria. Washington appointed three men to be commissioners. They were to live somewhere near the district and supervise the work that was soon to begin.

He hired Pierre-Charles L'Enfant, a Frenchman who had fought under him during the Revolution, to plan the city. L'Enfant's mind reeled with grand ideas. His father had been an artist for the French king, and L'Enfant had grown up at the palace at Versailles. He knew how a city grand enough for Washington's dreams ought to be built.

While the roads were still frozen, and before they turned to impassable mud, George Washington made the three-day trip by carriage from Philadelphia to the federal district. He met with L'Enfant and the three commissioners on a dank and chilly March day in Suter's Fountain Inn at Georgetown.

A thick mist hung over the area as the men left the inn at the edge of the federal district. Even on a bright day the men would have seen only low, rolling hills and the scattered buildings of twenty-nine farms in the area that is now downtown Washington, D.C. David Burnes's small farmhouse perched a safe distance above Goose Creek. On the ridge was a steep-roofed farmhouse belonging to the Peerce family, its front yard full of the family graves. The only road was the ruts that had been made by farm wagons. The men forded Rock Creek carefully because the water was running fast.

Most of the men saw swampy places along the rivers and the many streams that flowed through the area, open fields, some thick forests, and a high place that the local farmers called Jenkins's Hill. Had they known what L'Enfant was seeing, they might have avoided a future problem.

Pierre-Charles L'Enfant never did understand that the trappings of royalty did not fit in with this new kind of democratic government that the Americans wanted. He thought of George Washington as a sort of elected king. And so when he looked at Jenkins's Hill, he pictured it as the perfect spot for his majestic white Congress building. He saw wide avenues of handsome office buildings and parks with monuments of heroes. In his mind the soggy land at the foot of Jenkins's Hill became fountains and pools.

The President's Palace, he told the men, ought to sit here on a ridge where it could be seen down the Potomac from twenty miles away. George Washington stopped him right there. He wanted the President's House (he emphasized *House*) farther to the west. The men returned to Suter's Fountain Inn to warm their chilly bones, and to give L'Enfant a chance to set down their ideas on paper.

Nine months later George Washington laid before Congress L'Enfant's plan for the city. It was magnificent. None of the congressmen had ever seen such a city, except for the few of them who had been to Paris.

On paper, Goose Creek was turned into a canal with a cascade of water at the foot of Jenkins's Hill. Everywhere in the public gardens were statues, columns, and obelisks. Wide avenues radiated outward from the Congress House and President's House like rays from a brilliant sun. Great terraces sloped from the public buildings down to the Potomac River.

How could a new country, still so poor that there was no money to pay the soldiers who had fought in the Revolution, ever find the money to build such a city? Thomas Jefferson and James Madison said it was too fancy, a plan for *châteaux*, the French word for castles. The President's House was grander than the king of England's palace! The house that L'Enfant had drawn on paper was five times larger than the house that was actually built for the president. The avenues were the widest ever known in America.

George Washington defended L'Enfant as long as he could. The architect was talented but very headstrong. He would take no orders from anyone except the president himself, and Washington was often busy running the country from Philadelphia when decisions had to be made on-site in the federal district.

L'Enfant was in no hurry to build the city. He wanted it to grow slowly through many years, and could see no reason to rush. He could not understand when the president told him he might not be reelected, and a new president with different ideas would come into office. Surely Washington would be president for life?

The last straw came in February 1792. After much urging from everyone, L'Enfant had still not given the com-

L'Enfant's map, engraved by Andrew Ellicott, was published in the above magazine just a month after L'Enfant was fired. (*Library of Congress*)

missioners the completed map they wanted. The government needed to sell the lots on the city plan in order to have enough money to build the Congress House, the President's House, and the other public buildings. To the great relief of the commissioners, Washington fired L'Enfant.

The job of surveying the city lots now fell to Andrew Ellicott, who had been hired by George Washington to lay the boundaries of the ten-mile square, assisted by Benjamin Banneker, a free black man with a genius for mathematics and astronomy. Ellicott used L'Enfant's city plan, with a few changes. But now there was no real architect to design the important buildings. Thomas Jefferson suggested holding a national contest, with the winners to be chosen by the middle of July.

No famous architects volunteered for the contest. Only

nine drawings were submitted, and none of those were from Philadelphia or New York. The architects in those two cities were saving themselves for the day that this idea of building a federal city in the wilderness collapsed. Then the Congress would have to choose one of their cities instead.

The men who did compete to design the President's House had no idea what sort of rooms were needed. One drew a reception hall with a draped throne for the president. Another drew a plantation house.

One man, James Hoban, went to Philadelphia and had a short visit with George Washington. He learned that the president liked bowed windows because they let in more light. He preferred a plain-style of stone house, not brick. And Hoban discovered that when Washington received visitors, his guests always stood in an oval with him, the president, standing by the fireplace. Having done his homework, Hoban designed a stone house, added some bowed windows and an oval-shaped room, and won the contest. He also got the job.

No winner was chosen yet for the Congress House, even though sixteen designs had been submitted, one of them by a "Mr. AZ." He turned out to be Thomas Jefferson, but his design was rejected as too ornate.

Lear sat entranced listening as George Washington brought him up to date on the building of the federal city that his pamphlet was to describe to the American people. But later, when Lear moved to his writing desk and dipped his quill into the ink, the magic had gone. He wished he could recapture Washington's excitement, but this pamphlet had to be filled with facts, not fancy.

Lear had a thick packet of notes from surveyors, merchants, fishermen, farmers, boat captains, and dozens of other men he had questioned for ideas. But the hard fact

Two of the losing designs for the U.S. Capitol. James Diamond topped his with his own idea of an eagle, while Philip Hart borrowed the idea of placing "people" on the high spots from British castle architects. (*The National Archives*)

TERMS of SALE of LOTS in the CITY of WASH-
INGTON, the Eighth Day of *October*, 1792.

ALL Lands purchafed at this Sale, are to be fubject to the Terms and
Conditions declared by the Prefident, purfuant to the Deeds in
Truft.

The purchafer is immediately to pay one fourth part of the purchafe
money; the refidue is to be paid in three equal annual payments, with yearly
intereft of fix per cent. on the whole principal unpaid : If any payment is
not made at the day, the payments made are to be forfeited, or tne whole
principal and intereft unpaid may be recovered on one fuit and execution,
in the option of the Commiffioners.

The purchafer is to be entitled to a conveyance, on the whole purchafe
money and intereft being paid, and not before. No bid under Three
Dollars to be received.

A handbill to sell lots in the new federal city, 1792 (*Library of Congress*)

remained that ten thousand lots had to be sold for $240
each, although the price rose quickly before the first auction
in 1791. Lear's book had to make men want to buy lots at
what was then a very high price and set up their businesses
and manufacturing companies. Otherwise the first president's dream city could still be a failure.

The new government needed money at once. The time
had come to start building the public buildings—at least a
house for the president to live in, another where Congress
could meet, a treasury, war department, and who knew
what other buildings. A "superb Hotel," still only imaginary,
was to be paid for by lottery.

And now a deadline had been set. George Washington
ordered that all of the government workers and president
must move from Philadelphia into the new city by the fall
of 1800.

Lear decided that safety must be on the minds of men
who might buy the land. After all, cities too near the seacoast

were in danger of being invaded by the enemy in case of war, but that did not threaten this city. He dipped his quill into the ink and wrote.

"Not a river in America is capable of being rendered more secure of an attack by water than the Potowmack," he wrote confidently. (The British were to prove him wrong in 1814.) Then he told his readers that, unlike all other cities in the world, the new federal city could never burn down. All its houses had to be built of either brick or stone, and were therefore fireproof. Nor would its streets cave in without warning, as some in Philadelphia and New York had done because homeowners had extended their basements by burrowing deep under the city streets. And where most cities had narrow streets with just enough space for wagons and coaches to pass safely, the streets in the new city were to be at least ninety feet across. Sidewalks were to be wide and not cluttered, as they were in most cities, where steps and cellar doors stuck out across the walkways.

As Lear warmed up to his subject, he thought of the ship traffic. No city could grow unless it had a seaport. Heavy ships now loaded at Alexandria. Smaller ones could sail upstream to Georgetown. But the finest harbor was to be on the eastern branch of the Potomac, where a long wharf was built out into deep water.

Not far away, Lear wrote, were white pine trees that would make perfect ship masts. The bases of the trees were six feet across, and not even a branch grew out of the trunk for a hundred feet up. That was the kind of detail that thrilled shipbuilders from the Old World, as Lear knew it would. Tall trees had disappeared from Europe centuries before. The white pines he spoke of were actually about two hundred miles upriver from the new city, but Lear imagined that small detail would be no problem as soon as engineers built a few canals.

When Tobias Lear wrote his pamphlet about the new Washington City, this dock in Georgetown suddenly became a crowded landing place. (*Library of Congress*)

Right now, boats could not continue up the Potomac past Georgetown. Four miles above the federal city was the Little Falls, where the Patowmack Company, once headed by George Washington, was building a canal with three locks to go around the rapids. Ten miles farther up the river was the Great Falls where the canal would soon have six locks. George Washington had built his greatest hopes on the canal around the falls. He was sure a great deal of traffic would use the upper part of the river.

"The Great Advantage is the opening to the West," Lear wrote. For years the people who took flatboats from Pittsburgh (in Pennsylvania) down the Ohio and Mississippi rivers had had no good way to get home from New Orleans. "Now," wrote Lear, "they could sail back to the east coast and up the Potomac River to the federal city, take a canalboat another hundred and eighty miles to Cumberland, then take a forty-mile wagon road (if they could find a horse), take another boat north on the Monongahela River, and when they reached Pittsburgh, start down the Ohio River, and make the trip all over again." Obviously Lear had never tried this "Great Advantage" tour himself. Neither did anyone else, as it would have added about four months to the trip back to Pittsburgh.

Lear's pamphlet may not have impressed flatboaters and other western adventurers, but he did make the city look good on paper. He attracted business, and the lots began to sell.

Although the commissioners named the federal district the territory of Columbia, the city was officially named Washington on 9 September 1791.

2

A City Comes to Life

"Thank God he [George Washington] can ride in a carriage that is not bulletproof!"

—Benjamin More, newspaper editor, 1796

Washington City sounded a great deal finer in Lear's pamphlet than it looked in real life.

On the day people bought Lear's publication, the capital city's streets were still outlined by surveyors' stakes. The only buildings, aside from the farm buildings, were wooden shacks set up to shelter the workers and carpentry shops. Where grand avenues were promised, rutted dirt roads cut around orchards and fields. Thick forests of oak, sycamore, and cedar still sheltered wolves and bears.

For a while, after L'Enfant left, the work slowed. The problem was that no one actually knew how to build a house with large stone blocks. Stonemasons refused to come from the larger cities. They had good jobs where they were, and each thought his own city might still be chosen as the capital as soon as this "federal city" idea failed. Neither did they want to leave their families behind, and they could not bring them. There were no homes for them to live in, no churches, not even a decent general store, except in nearby Georgetown.

John Suter, of the Fountain Inn, wrote a letter to Scotland to tell his cousin Collen Williamson, who was a stonemason, to come at once. Suter's letter took months to reach Scotland, and summer arrived before Williamson came to take over as master mason.

On a Saturday in fall, Williamson and the commissioners laid the cornerstone for the President's House. Today, almost two hundred years later, no one has been able to find that same cornerstone with its eight-inch brass plate that was pressed into the wet mortar. Scientists tried hunting for it with everything from a mine detector to X-ray machines, without success. For the record, this is what it says:

THIS FIRST STONE OF THE PRESIDENT'S HOUSE WAS LAID THE 13TH DAY OF OCTOBER 1792, AND IN THE SEVENTEENTH YEAR OF THE INDEPENDENCE OF THE UNITED STATES OF AMERICA

GEORGE WASHINGTON, PRESIDENT

THOMAS JEFFERSON
DOCTOR STEWART
DANIEL CARROLL
COMMISSIONERS

JAMES HOBAN, ARCHITECT
COLLEN WILLIAMSON, MASTER MASON

VIVAT REPUBLICA
(LONG LIVE THE REPUBLIC)

When Thomas Jefferson asked the commissioners where they hoped to find construction workers, he received this answer:

> "People are tip Toe [eager] to come from all parts. We might probably have two thousand mechanics and labourers here on very short notice."

But the mechanics and skilled laborers failed to show up. Instead, the commissioners had to hire slaves from their masters for twenty-one pounds a year, plus their food. (Naturally the money went to the masters, not the slaves.) Each master sent his slaves with clothing and one blanket each. When it was too cold to work on construction in the winter, the slaves cleared the many stumps and trees from the streets. Eight years later, the stumps still had not all been pulled out.

Williamson called for more stonecutters, especially since it began to look as if they would be building the Congress House as well as that of the president. One entire Masonic lodge group of stonecutters came from Scotland, bringing along their own Presbyterian minister. They moved into twenty small, unpainted wood cottages nailed together hastily.

The Scots did not like the idea of training slaves in the trade they had worked many years to learn, especially since the slaves were owned by others and would later be sent out to compete with them for jobs. They insisted on hiring young white apprentices instead. But the other workmen used the slave labor.

The brickyard for all the public buildings was set up at the President's House. Slaves made bricks from the clay soil, mixing the soil with sand brought from the creeks. The master brickmaker, Jeremiah Kale, could tell by tasting the clay with his tongue when the mixture was just right. He knew when the kilns had been heated to just the right temperature to bake the bricks. For five years, Kale's workers turned out five thousand bricks a day.

Slaves dug the building stone about forty miles down the Potomac at Aquia Creek, and later from the hillsides on Mount Vernon land. Only after the moist stone dried did it become hard. Then it turned color. Later, the stonemasons discovered that the stones soaked up water when it rained. After the first freeze, they found that ice had formed inside the stones. When the ice expanded, the stones began to crack open. To prevent this, the stones had to be sealed with a whitewash, thus making the President's House a startling white color.

Spain made an unexpected contribution to the President's House when a Spanish ship was captured and taken into Norfolk harbor. Its cargo was a large quantity of fine mahogany.

Very soon after Lear's pamphlet went on sale in bookshops in every city, the capital city began to change. Farmer David Burnes, however, was still stubbornly planting his cornfields in what was fast becoming the middle of the city. Burnes had not wanted to sell his land, but George Washington called on him one day to talk to him about it. What Washington had to say, and what Burnes had to answer, is told a hundred different ways, as are most stories about the first president. The facts are that the next time Burnes planted his corn, the commissioners went ahead and cut Pennsylvania Avenue through the middle of his field.

The city now had a hotel called the Great Hotel, or Blodget's. The first visitors, including one named James Kent, came out of curiosity to see what was going on. Kent,

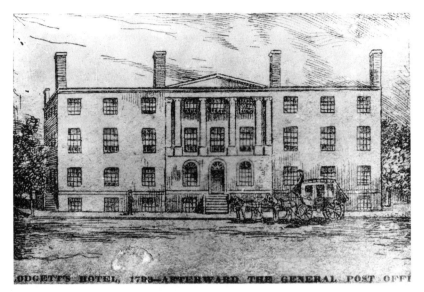

Washington's first grand hotel was Blodget's, begun in 1793. Later it became the General Post Office, the home of the Patent Office, and in 1814 was the only building large enough to house the Congress for a short time. (*National Archives*)

like all the tourists who came to see the federal city, walked through the President's House to see how it looked. "The Basement Story was laid and built of greyish white free Stone handsomely polished," he wrote in his diary.

The three commissioners were now paid for their work and told they must live in the new city, and not in George-town where life was much more comfortable. One of the commissioners, Dr. William Thornton, had designed the Capitol building and needed to be on hand every day now that it was under construction.

Part of the commissioners' job was to sell lots in the city. In the federal city, lots were described by their "numbers." Usually when a person bought a lot in this country, a sur-veyor measured his property from one tree to another, but in the new city the trees were being cut down fast. No one but the surveyor knew where the city streets were supposed to go, and so buyers could not be given an address. They identified their lots by numbers only.

A buyer was supposed to build a house on his lot as soon as possible, but that was easier said than done. All the construction workers were busily employed putting up the federal buildings. A new lot owner who wanted to build a shop or a tavern, so he could go into business and begin making money, had such a hard time finding carpenters that often he had to give up. Some traveled miles from the city to hire their own workmen. Others went bankrupt and could not pay for their property, and so their lots were sold again.

One of the first houses built in the city was a double one, built by George Washington. On 4 January Dr. and Mrs. William Thornton went to see the two joined houses. "They are divided," Anna Maria Thornton wrote in her diary, "so as to be let [rented] as one house or two houses."

In June 1796, Benjamin More arrived at the city, rented a building from John Crocker, and started a newspaper called the *Washington Gazette*. The paper came out twice a week, on Wednesdays and Saturdays.

"This is the only paper printed in the City of Washington," Editor More wrote, almost as if he suspected that a few years later another publisher would claim that *his* newspaper was the first.

More's newspaper was the first glimpse into the unfinished city as it began coming to life. A hat manufactory now stood on Square 86, and a nail manufactory at Greenleaf Point. More reported that on Square 651 "very spirited exertions are making to erect a number of brick houses." John Thomas's bookshop, next to McKnight's Tavern, brought culture to the city by adding violins, stationery, flutes, and guitars to his line of books. The first child born in Wash-

GEORGE WASHINGTON'S HOUSE IN WASHINGTON.
(BUILT BY HIM IN 1792.)

One of the first houses completed in Washington City was this two-family home built by George Washington in 1792. He never lived here but rented it as an income property. (*The National Archives*)

ington died, without leaving even its name behind. Slavery was everywhere. At a public sale "Two Valuable Negroes, a girl about sixteen and a boy nine, both accustomed to house work," were sold at a good price.

But not all black people were slaves. From the start of

the capital city, Washington was known as the "freest place in the South" for black people to live. Some came as slaves and earned their own freedom by working to build the Capitol, the Navy Yard, and other buildings. Unlike the surrounding southern states, Washington City had no laws requiring free black people to leave the district after a certain length of stay. Free blacks, and many escaped slaves posing as free, found jobs of every sort and fit well into the young city.

James Sweeney owned a grocery very close to the President's House. Sweeney sold everything from feathers, beads, and "India garbs" to brown sugar, candles, hair powder, and diaper tablecloths. But to buy medicine, the townspeople had to travel to Frederick Miller's apothecary shop in Georgetown.

Crime arrived early at the new city. The tools bought by the commissioners for the builders disappeared almost as soon as they arrived. Someone got into the carriage shop and cut up the lining of Mr. Fitzhugh's chariot. He had a blacksmith arrested on suspicion. And a man who called himself "Jeremiah Eaton" was wanted for forgery. A huge $200 reward was offered for Eaton, who was five foot eight and one-half inches tall and squarely built, with blue eyes and a dark complexion. Eaton should be easy to spot, said the newspaper, because "he speaks quickly and in general boasts much of his property and business."

The newspaper editor enjoyed most comparing his former ruler, King George III, with his present leader. His Majesty's stagecoach had just undergone some alterations in London. The glass in its sides and back had been replaced with heavy panels, and lined with musket-proof sheet copper "for the better protection of his majesty's sacred person." Then More added that George Washington had just arrived in Washington City on August 13, 1796. "Thank God," he wrote, "he can ride in a carriage that is not bulletproof!"

On Sundays, Washington City was quiet. Townspeople and workers attended church services at the unpainted wooden carpenter's hall at first. Then a Roman Catholic church, St. Patrick's, was built of plain wood. The minister of the Scottish stonemasons had already built a wooden St. Andrew's to keep his small flock in line. The Scots, whose Sundays at home forbid even a laugh or an idle moment, were often shocked at the way Southerners in the United States visited friends and had fun with their children on Sundays.

During George Washington's last term the builders began to put up some of the office buildings. Everyone, especially those who had bought property on Jenkins's Hill, expected that all the federal offices would be built near the Congress House. But the president had other ideas. He wanted the Treasury Department and the War Office near the President's House. One day he arrived in the city and by himself staked out the sites for those buildings.

With the end of George Washington's terms as president came a sort of relief that all had gone well with the new government. Washington, himself, had been very careful not to set any wrong precedents for the presidents who followed him. Especially during the first years he kept questioning himself and others whose advice he trusted. Should a president have a title? Should he be available all the time to the public? Did his advisers think he should have a coat of arms painted on his coach?

At first the Title Committee of the Senate had just about settled on this mouthful for his title: "His Highness, the President of the United States of America, and Protector of the Rights of the Same." Then Senator MacClay of Pennsylvania reminded the others that the Constitution said, "No title of nobility shall be granted by the United States." The House of Representatives was dead set against any title at all, except plain *President.*

This horrified John Adams, who had always felt the presidency should be more like royalty. He spoke to the Senate for forty minutes and ended with this:

> "What will the common people of foreign countries, what will the sailors and the soldiers say, 'George Washington, President of the United States?' They will despise him to all eternity."

MacClay's answer to Adams had been:

> "What the common people, soldiers and sailors of foreign countries may think of us, I do not think it imports us much. Perhaps, the less they think or have occasion to think of us, the better."

And yet many people felt as Adams did. Among them were some senators who still thought of the Senate as very much like the British House of Lords, while the House of Representatives was equal to the British House of Commons, and therefore the lower house. George Washington understood that the men in Congress had grown up with this feeling planted deeply within them, but he did not approve of it. For that reason, he came down hard on the builders when it appeared that they were going to finish the Senate part of the Capitol building long before the House of Representatives. He insisted that the entire Capitol and the President's House must be finished in time for the opening of the business session of Congress and transfer of the federal government from Philadelphia to the new capital in November of 1800.

George Washington had a special way of saying "I require it" that left no room for argument. His ideas for finishing the house, even though he would never live in it, included a grand staircase made of stone, not wood. He "required" that the roof be made of slate, and that they use wood rather than stone for the main floor.

Ten days after John Adams was inaugurated as president, but months before the Adams family had moved to the city, George Washington stopped at the President's House on his way home to Mount Vernon. With him were his wife, Martha, his stepdaughter Nelly Custis, and young George Washington Lafayette. The boy's parents, the marquis de Lafayette, who had fought for American independence, and his wife, were then in a French prison.

The family went to a large banquet given in Washington's honor near the Capitol building. Then they drove past the President's House. The crowds had not been allowed to attend the banquet, so they had all gathered at the White House, knowing that the president must drive past. The slates for the roof had not yet arrived, and the carpenter had not built the wooden frames for the windows, but the White House had a certain air about it that pleased him. Captain James Hoban stood in front with his Washington Artillery Company and ordered a sixteen-gun salute. That was the only ceremony of any kind at the President's House ever attended by George Washington.

Just before Christmas, on 14 December 1799, Washington died at Mount Vernon. After his funeral, the city declared his birthday to be a day of mourning.

Anna Maria, wife of Dr. Thornton, was shocked that some of her younger friends attended a ball at Tunnicliffe's

Tavern on 5 February, "so near the day appointed for a day of mourning." Three weeks after his death, Congress started planning a huge mausoleum for Washington's body. His wife, Martha, consented to have his body moved to the city named for him, and a secret vote in Congress included space for Martha to lie in it beside him after she died.

In February, George Washington's birthday ceremony was held in Mr. McCormich's church on New Jersey Avenue, with a procession at 2:00 P.M. Another service was held in the afternoon in Georgetown. "The people of the city and Georgetown joined to shew their respect for the late General Washington," said Mrs. Thornton, "but the society is too small for them to equal in pomp the other cities. But they did their best. There were about one thousand people assembled at the church."

3

What the Inspectors Saw

"... went to the Capitol ... while Dr. Thornton laid out an oval, round which is to be the communication to the Gallery of the Senate Room. ..."
—Anna Maria Thornton in January 1800

The carriage of President John Adams pulled slowly away from the Executive Mansion in Philadelphia on 27 May 1800. Inside was John Adams and a favorite nephew, William Shaw. The young man, who had just graduated from Harvard, was to serve as the president's secretary during the summer. His job began with this trip to inspect the new city of Washington.

The president's coach sparkled as the morning sun reflected off the silver-mounted harness of the horses. The Adamses' coach was known well in Philadelphia. His footmen, dressed in bright livery, made the coach hard *not* to notice. Some people, however, may have also noticed that the handsome coat of arms, once painted on the side of the coach, was no longer there.

John Adams felt the president of the United States should

For John Adams, following a popular president like George Washington was not easy. (*Library of Congress*)

live somewhat like a king and conduct himself with regal dignity. Adams's servants and many others addressed him as Your Excellency. He greeted his guests with a stiff bow from the waist. But he knew the people did not love and revere him the way they had worshiped George Washington. Americans had a dread of anything that suggested royalty to them—like a castle, a title, bowing and curtsying, or even a coat of arms. And so Adams had had the colorful painting removed from his coach.

Philadelphia, on this day, was looking like a ghost town. Its streets were filled with cartloads of furniture as one member of Congress after another moved his family out of their temporary dwellings in the city that had been the capital for ten years. Many were headed home for the summer. Others, who had not yet found space to live in the federal city, had to go there first or they would have no roof over their heads when the fall term began in November, soon after election day.

Adams's coach driver did not take the regular road from Philadelphia through Baltimore and on to Washington City. The president had decided to make a circle tour—west to the towns of Lancaster and York and through some smaller villages where voters lived. To Adams, campaigning for re-election was a distasteful job, but it had to be done. George Washington had been elected to office for two terms, and John Adams intended to be also.

Adams was pleased with his visit to the smaller cities. Crowds had lined the narrow roads and cheered, although none had taken off their shoes as a mark of respect, as they would have done for a king, and as some old soldiers had once done for their general, Washington. Adams and Shaw were invited to dinners, troops of horsemen met them outside the towns, church bells rang, and citizens illuminated their homes by lighting a candle in every window. A good road had carried them to Lancaster, and all had gone well until the coach driver turned toward the south. Then, somewhere beyond the town of Frederick, in Maryland, all traces of road and of bridges over streams vanished.

There was not yet an official map of the road to Washington City, although any stagecoach driver or wagon master could have told the Adams party they had made a large mistake not going by the well-traveled road through Baltimore. That road had only a few long stretches through wilderness where a person had to worry about highway robbers. Most of it was lined by miles of prickly hawthorn fences, hard for robbers to hide in. On that road, taverns were plentiful, with cheerful names like the Swan, the Wheatsheaf, the Practical Farmer, the Grand Turk, and the Bird in Hand.

The Adams party discovered their mistake soon enough. The footmen had to climb up on the coach roof, hacking and chopping at branches until their new uniforms were in tatters. The coach driver finally located a faint wagon path. They followed it, dodging tree stumps and even full grown trees in the path's center. The passengers banged against each other, feeling as if their insides were being totally rearranged. Not a single tavern appeared to offer a chance to stop for something to eat or drink. They were grateful for only one advantage—this wilderness was so far from civilization that they did not see a single robber. The trip that Adams thought would take only four days lasted for eight.

Bruised and sore they arrived on 3 June at the new Union Tavern in Georgetown. The next day the long-awaited tour of the capital began.

The city's commissioners, Gustavus Scott, Alexander White, and Dr. William Thornton, rode on horseback to

The only road from Georgetown shows the traveler's first view of the new city of Washington in 1804. (*Library of Congress*)

show the city to Adams and Shaw. The road from Georgetown to the President's House was only two miles long, but it proved no better than those they had jostled over the past several days. The carriage moved through potholes of sticky mud, and crossed Rock Creek on a crude plank bridge.

The stark white of the President's House stood out in the distance, as startling in this wild place as a king's palace might have been. Looking off in every direction, Adams and Shaw found it hard to imagine that a real city would be here some day. A few dwelling houses, including that of the stubborn farmer David Burnes, miles of land covered with scrub oak bushes, and a great deal of swamp looked all the more forlorn because of the great White House. The commissioners pointed proudly to the "Six Buildings" and the larger "Seven Buildings," two rows of brick houses on the same street as the President's House.

At last the group neared the huge sandstone building that was soon to be the Adamses' home. Depending on how the election went, he and Abigail might have to live in it another four years.

The carriage driver hesitated at the entrance to the north door of the house. Heavy planks half covered a deep pit separating the house from the drive. A workman waved frantically at the driver, signaling him to approach the house by another route. Finally the coach stopped before a door that led into the cellar.

Adams and Shaw balanced carefully on boards that had been thrown down across the larger mud puddles and edged around piles of rubble near the basement entrance. The company of men with them dismounted and followed the two through the doorway.

Inside, the basement had been whitewashed and the wood painted white. The floor was orange brick paving stones. The kitchen was huge, and would probably need an army of cooks. A workman pointed toward the only set of steps in the building, and the visitors groped their way in the dark up a narrow, twisting stairway that rose from basement to attic.

On the main floor of the huge building, where John and Abigail Adams were to spend the coming winter, the president found matters not much better. The ceilings were twice as high as any he had ever seen on this side of the Atlantic Ocean. A wagoner could have driven his team of horses down the hallway without bumping into the new doors, all of which were leaning against the walls. An embarrassed workman explained that the doors could not be hung until the new door handles came.

"The new wallpaper has not come yet from Philadelphia, either," he added, when the inspectors glanced upward at the ugly walls. Only half the rooms had been plastered, and the rank smell of wet plaster was everywhere. Although it was already a warm June day, fires blazed in every room to dry out the walls.

Joseph and Electius Middleton, the carpenters, had moved their entire workshop into the President's House, and were now hammering in the wooden window frames. Other workers were installing ready-made plaster ornaments that had been bought to attach to the ceiling and to decorate the wall panels.

The three commissioners hovered in the background while Adams looked around. He was not a warm, friendly man under the best of conditions. The first explosion came when he caught sight of an ugly mantelpiece in the room intended for his office. For a few minutes he stood motionless, staring at the carving in front of him. One of the commissioners hurried forward.

"The carving represents man and beast," he explained.

Adams said he would not live in the same house with it. The men all agreed the carving should be changed at once to something more suitable, like urns or flowers.

Then Adams discovered there were no household bells to call the servants. Surely in a house this size, the president was not expected to shout down the winding stairway to raise one of them! The commissioners looked surprised. Bells to ring for servants were quite modern. They had not thought of them but promised to attend to them at once.

The president also insisted on a vegetable garden, with herbs to use for medicine. Dr. Thornton volunteered to plant the garden himself. Then came the question of furniture. Adams said he had not enough chairs in the Philadelphia house, and this home was going to need dozens more.

When the president asked about the huge gaping hole in the center of the hall, the commissioners told him that some day the great stone stairway would be there. Until then everyone, president and servants alike, would have to use the narrow winding stairs.

Only a few years before, the Republicans had claimed this President's House was nothing but a "Federalist palace." As Adams looked around him he knew that no one could accuse him of having royal ideas living in this drafty barn, filled with the worn-out government furniture he would soon be moving into it.

Back in the carriage again, the party continued its tour. Only a few of the public buildings were completed, because no one had yet decided how large they ought to be. Nor had they agreed on where to put them all. The Treasury building and War Office, though, stood where George Washington had staked out their sites.

The Treasury building was not finished. The only treasure in it so far was the portrait that Gilbert Stuart had painted of the first president. The State Department was almost finished.

A small crisis developed over where the president's stable ought to go. Finally a brick one was built two blocks away; stables smelled too bad to be near a nice home.

The carriage and riders turned into Pennsylvania Avenue. Far ahead, sitting white and proud on top of Jenkins's Hill, was one completed wing of the Congress House. Just as George Washington had feared, the senators' meeting place was finished first. Only the foundation had been dug for the second wing. The two wings were joined by a wooden porch, also temporary. The Supreme Court was to meet in a basement room.

Dr. Thornton had been given the job of completing the

Gilbert Stuart's painting of George Washington was in the Treasury building in 1800. It is the one that was rescued by Dolley Madison fourteen years later. (*Library of Congress*)

Just as President George Washington had feared, only the north, or Senate, wing of the Capitol had been completed by 1800. (*Library of Congress*)

Capitol. A man of many talents, he was a medical doctor as well as an architect, a city magistrate, and the head of the patent office. In January, he had laid out an oval for the workers to build. This day he would show it proudly to the president, pointing out the entrance from it to the gallery of the Senate room.

As the carriage slowly rumbled toward the Capitol, Shaw kept looking at a copy of the federal city map L'Enfant had made several years before. The map did not look anything like the "city" they saw around them. On the parchment, Pennsylvania Avenue was wide and elegant. But when the carriage detoured up a muddy slope heading for the Capitol building, the inspectors saw that the grand "avenue" was a swamp for almost its entire length. One "park" was still an apple orchard. The streets were still just rows of surveyors' stakes, with tough old tree stumps and alder bushes growing in the center.

From the Capitol building down toward the east branch of the Potomac River was a wide dirt road called New Jersey Avenue. Two government buildings stood on one side of the avenue, and one on the other. A fourth building was the huge brick house of Daniel Carroll, one of the earliest commissioners, and a longtime friend of George Washington.

Carroll had built his home before the surveyors laid out the street, and so it rose in the middle of the avenue. In the old days, he might have gotten away with it and had the route of the avenue changed. But in this new country, the laws were meant to apply equally to the gentry and the poor. L'Enfant had ordered Carroll's house torn down, and Washington had ordered it rebuilt at once—but in its proper place.

For ten days Adams and Shaw toured Washington City, staying at Tunnicliffe's new hotel and city tavern on the "Great Post Road" near Maryland Avenue. In spite of what must have seemed a hopeless construction muddle, the city was beginning to bustle with life.

Three sloops arrived at Lear's Wharf (Tobias Lear had now gone into the import and export business) with loads of government papers while Adams was there. The heavy traffic of hauling goods from wharf to offices kicked up dust that hung over the city.

Adams and Shaw had both survived serious epidemics of yellow fever in Philadelphia caused, they believed, by just such dust and exposure to ships from foreign ports as they saw in this new city. A person had to bathe quickly to cleanse his skin and open the pores without enfeebling his body, because cleanliness was the grand preservative against the diseases of the season. Then, even on the hottest days, every person wore flannel next to the skin to keep disease from entering the body through its pores. Housewives washed their floors often and threw pails of water on the pavement in front of the door in the morning before the sun was on it so the yellow fever could not find a footing there. But here there was no pavement. And everywhere were puddles of water. Trees were being cut down instead of planted. Didn't the city builders know that the vibration of the trees purified the air and kept the yellow fever from areas where there were parks?

And everywhere there were crowds—another sure way to spread deadly fevers. Taverns bulged with congressmen, secretaries, and politicians who had come to find places to live during the next session of Congress. Inns like the Little Hotel, "near the Treasury and for Gentlemen Travelers," had already rented out all their rooms for the next year. Almost every home offered space for boarders—at a high price.

The mail coach stopped at Tunnicliffe's Hotel every day except Sunday. There was no faster way to return to Philadelphia than by mail coach. The post drivers were a swaggering breed of men, famous for their skill and knowledge. A driver had to sign a contract promising he would arrive at each mail stop at a certain time or else pay a one-dollar fine for every fifteen minutes he was late. Only unavoidable accidents, such as a wheel falling off or a mail coach overturning, were excused. The mail coach picked up passengers at Tunnicliffe's at 8:00 A.M. About every ten miles, the driver stopped for fresh horses, but the change of horses was so fast the passengers had no time even to get outside the coach. On a rainy day, they often sat under or on top of the all-important mailbags. The mail came first in the post driver's mind. Carrying wet and uncomfortable passengers bothered him not in the least. But the mailbags must never get wet.

Nine hours later, at 5:00 P.M., the stiff and cramped passengers arrived at Evans Tavern in Baltimore. The tavernkeeper there provided some sort of dinner, for a high price. He had no competition because the mail coach passengers had no other place they could sleep. Only rarely did a passenger get a bed to himself. Usually he shared it, and the one brown sheet, with another traveler. He counted himself lucky if the stranger did not sleep with his boots and greatcoat on. As for fleas in the bed, every tavern had its own special brand.

Next morning the mail coach left Baltimore at whatever hour pleased the driver. The scheduled time was 3:00 A.M., but if the weather looked bad, the post driver called the passengers to be ready earlier so he would not have to pay the huge fine. Nineteen hours later, at 10:00 P.M., the exhausted passengers stumbled into Hardy's Inn, Philadephia.

President Adams, anxious to leave for the healthier climate of New England and home, had his coachman follow the mail stage route when they left Washington in the middle of June, although he and Shaw did not try to travel so fast. They had invitations to stay in private homes and so avoided the crowded and flea-ridden taverns. The trip to Philadelphia took them close to four days. After seven more days of travel and short rests, they reached Quincy, Massachusetts, early in July.

The Adamses Move In

". . . the best of blessings on this house and all that shall hereafter inhabit it."

—President John Adams in 1800

The road to and from Lear's Wharf was soon packed down hard. It was full of ruts and holes, but solid as rock. Wagoners and carters toted boxes of valuables over it to the public buildings all summer.

Families filed off the boats, with baggage and furniture and no idea where they would sleep that night. More families came in their own wagons. The city had nowhere near enough beds for them all.

Washington City now had six hundred houses, and most of those were temporary wooden ones. Twice six hundred would not have been enough. The citizens who opened boardinghouses preferred to take in congressmen as boarders, knowing they had come to stay for several months and not just a few days. Many government workers, knowing the conditions in the new city, had left their families at home.

"Our little party took lodging with a Mr. Peacock, in one of the houses on the New Jersey Avenue," said John Cotton Smith, a congressman from Connecticut. Speaker of the House Theodore Sedgwick was allowed a room to himself, but the other representatives had to share rooms at Peacock's.

"I do not perceive how the members of Congress can possibly secure lodgings," Oliver Wolcott, secretary of the treasury, wrote to his wife, "unless they will consent to live like scholars in a college, or monks in a monastery, crowded ten or twenty in one house."

Wolcott had finally found a room for himself over half a mile from his office. Back in New England, he could have walked the distance easily, but here there were no roads, no bridges to cross running water and marshes, and very few board sidewalks.

Like many other men of his day, Wolcott hated eating "a public dinner." That meant eating in a room with strangers—people he had not invited to dine with him. Even when they stayed at a tavern or hotel, most men sent their manservant to the kitchen to carry dinner up to them in their own rooms. Men from the more cultured parts of the United States could not bear to rub elbows at the table with men who dressed in buckskin and came from wilderness country. Such men helped themselves by plunging their knives into the butter or meat, then straight into their mouths, and back again to the community bowl for seconds and thirds. Many country people had never seen a fork.

Wolcott said he had never seen so many poor people, both white and free blacks. The city police counted 746 black people in the city, over 600 of them slaves. Wolcott felt his own life was so difficult in the new city that he could not imagine how the poor survived—nor did he really care.

It was not fashion able to worry about your poor neighbors in 1800.

"There are but few houses in any one place," he told his wife in a letter. "And most of them small miserable huts, which present an awful contrast to the public buildings." He thought a moment of the people he had seen, and then added, "As far as I can judge, they live like fishes, by eating each other."

Louisa Catharine, the wife of young John Quincy Adams, was shocked at everything she saw when she came to America from London. Country dress and manners, people who spoke with a nasal twang, dinners where one was served Indian pudding or boiled potatoes—all were foreign to her.

"Had I stepped into Noah's Ark, I do not think I could have been more utterly astonished," she said.

Among those who arrived in the city during the hot summer were two people very important to John and Abigail Adams. Esther and John Briesler had served the Adams family for many years. While Esther managed the housekeeping, John was the steward. But never, in all their service, had they faced such a host of problems as this new President's House gave them. Because there was no bedroom for the husband and wife, they slept in the basement storeroom where the best dishes were kept. All summer they prepared for the day when the Adamses moved into the White House.

One day during the summer of 1800, Lewis Beebe traveled to the city. Like most Americans of his day, he considered it his perfect right to wander through the President's House and other public buildings to see how they looked. Workmen were quite used to stepping around ladies and gentlemen. And the visitors were equally free with their

City surveyor Nicholas King drew this sketch of the President's House (on the hill, to left of center), as well as the house of Gales the newspaperman, the Patent Office (just above the ox's head), and, on the right, the former Blodget's Hotel that had just become the General Post Office. (*The National Archives*)

questions and advice on how the workmen ought to be doing their jobs.

"The Capitol is of stone," Beebe wrote in his diary that day. "Only one wing is built. The foundation for the other is laid. It is the most superb building I ever saw. The rooms are large and spacious, and adorned with the most beautiful skylights. When completed, it will make an amazing pile of building."

Beebe then rode his horse down Pennsylvania Avenue to check out the President's House. He was impressed to find carpets in every room, and "not an inch of wood used except in the doors and [window] sashes." Fortunately, he also described the unusual sewage system in the house in those years before the house was gutted by fire.

"The water that falls upon the house is received and carried by a tube through the center of the house, and discharged through a canal, and carried away underground."

Beebe also found the city crowded.

"There are more carriages and coachees and hacks in proportion to the number of inhabitants than I have ever seen," he marveled. "The removal of the government to here has caused a crowd of people to flow in like a torrent upon this city. Nearly two hundred are constantly employed in writing in the public offices. The mails from New York and Philadelphia arrive every day."

Prices were extremely high. Beebe paid five dollars a week for his room and board while he stayed in the city. He would have had to pay three hundred dollars to rent a small wooden house for a year, at a time when most people did not earn a hundred dollars in a year.

One plot of ground, between the President's House and the Potomac River, was high above the marshes, with a level surface on the top. There, Beebe said, a special mausoleum was to be built for George Washington. But Beebe was wrong. Both Martha and George Washington remain today buried at Mount Vernon, but many years after Beebe visited the city, the Washington Monument was built on that ground.

Any young man who wrote neatly could get a job in Washington City. A copy had to be made of every letter that was written, and the only way to make one was to have someone copy the letter down in a "letter book." Dr. Thornton was lucky; his wife made it her business to copy all his letters for him.

One of the favorite sports of the men who worked in the public offices was bird shooting. In his stationery shop at Georgetown, Michael Roberts sold a large assortment of sporting goods in addition to lamps, playing cards, German flutes, and tea kettles. He carried fowling pieces (for shooting birds), pistols, battle powder, shot, swords, travel pouches, and officers' camp equipage.

Every man owned a gun and needed only to walk as far as the nearby woods to bring home woodcocks and blackbirds to be made into potpies. The Potomac River gave city sportsmen plenty of rockfish for dinner and catfish for soup. On the Virginia side of the river, from October to April, gentlemen hunted fox, but not so they could put food on the table. They always took the fox alive to keep for the next hunt and went home to an elegant supper made and served by their slaves.

Lewis Beebe had often shot food for his own family back home, but he found it hard to understand why any man wanted to go leaping fences and across gullies after a fox. "You could be thrown from your horse and your brains dashed out," he said. Then added quickly, "One person always stays with the body, while the others finish the hunt."

All through the summer and early fall Washington City hummed with activity. New families and businesses moved in, and nobody moved out to make more space. Everyone was in a hurry to be ready by Monday, 17 November. On that day congressmen from all over the United States were to sit for the first time in the new Congress House.

One man working feverishly to be ready before that day was Samuel Harrison Smith. He had loaded his printing press, and everything else he needed to start a newspaper, onto a ship in Philadelphia at the end of September. For weeks after that day, he paced the wharf at Georgetown for word of the ship carrying his press.

One ship captain after another told him about the violent storms they had just gone through along the Atlantic coast.

At last word came from one sea captain who had seen Smith's ship. It had been driven on shore by the storm, he reported, but there was a chance it had not sunk. Just two weeks before Congress convened, a battered ship arrived at the dock with Smith's printing press aboard and the materials to set up the paper.

On Saturday morning, 1 November, the commissioners toured the President's House one last time. President John Adams arrived the same day. Abigail was not with him. She had been sick and promised to follow him as soon as she felt better.

Adams found his living quarters still unfinished. The yard around it was a disaster area. Piles of chipped building stones, rusting iron, broken roof slates, crumbling bricks, and rocks lay scattered about. Huge holes, dug out to mix clay bricks during the building process, had filled with muddy water. The only greenery, except for the garden Dr. Thornton planted, was the weeds. Nothing had been picked up except the wood, and it had all been burned to help dry out the plaster walls.

Two days later, Samuel Harrison Smith published the first issue of the *National Intelligencer and Washington Advertiser*. Benjamin More's earlier paper had not lasted long, or perhaps its editor had died. At any rate, Smith made the same claim that his newspaper was the first on the scene. "It is the first Paper printed in WASHINGTON," wrote editor Smith, "and from the vicinity of the Editor to the Capitol, the seat of the public bodies, he expects to be enabled to furnish the earliest and most correct notices of their deliberations."

Smith proved to be an unusual editor for his day. No one owned him. He believed in the "sacred duties" of the press to report everything just as he heard it. This American way of treating the important men who ran the country was unheard of. Until now, newspaper editors published anonymous letters to criticize the government or an important person. No one had yet written a newspaper to "tell it like it is" from the very seat of government. "TRUTH and truth only, shall be the guide of the Editor," Smith promised in his first edition.

Smith's newspaper went so far as to predict the outcome of the election to be held 11 November. The campaign had been the dirtiest so far, and Adams had only five states in his favor. Eight states were lined up behind Thomas Jefferson and Aaron Burr. Three states were still undecided.

Smith's paper had little to say about John Adams's arrival in town, except that the "President of the U.S. arrived in this city and took up his residence in the house appropriated to him by the commissioners."

Before Adams went to bed that first night in the house, he sat down to write a letter to Abigail. "Before I end my letter," he concluded, "I pray Heaven to bestow the best of blessings on this house and all that shall hereafter inhabit it. May none but wise and honest men ever rule under this roof."

Curious Happenings:
A Free Press and a
Strange Election

> "The great unfinished Audience room, I make a drying room to hang up the clothes in."
>
> —Abigail Adams in 1800

The president's first week was not an easy one. First came Oliver Wolcott. That unhappy man had never liked the city and had resigned as secretary of the treasury. Samuel Dexter, the former secretary of war, took his place.

Before the week was over, the "fireproof" city had its first large fire. A three-story building, used temporarily by the War Department, burned to the ground. With it went many important papers, as well as a valuable library of books on the tactics of fighting a war.

Abigail Adams arrived at her new home on Sunday, 16 November, the day before Congress was to open. Traveling with nine people, the new coachman had taken the wrong road out of Baltimore. Soon they ran into deep woods. Their carriage and wagons had gone a half day's journey before they realized they had not yet crossed the Patapsco River as they should have. They had passed a few small cottages "without a single glass window" but had not seen a single human. In every direction there was a solid wall of trees. "We wandered two hours without finding a guide or the path," Abigail wrote to her daughter later. "Fortunately, a straggling black came up with us and we engaged him as a guide to extricate us out of our difficulty."

Abigail's exhaustion was not all caused by the journey. She had stopped in New York to visit their second son. Young Charles Adams had once been a happy, carefree boy, the life of every family gathering. Now he was a drunk. He had deserted his wife and two small daughters, only to return to them a year later, when he was very sick. When Abigail had left his bedside in New York on her way to Washington, she knew she would never see her son again. He was dying.

The Adamses were a warm, close family. Their daughter, Abigail, always called Nabby, had married and given them grandchildren. Son John Quincy had become a Boston lawyer and was now a foreign minister to Prussia. Their youngest son, Thomas Boylston, was studying at Harvard and was soon to go to Philadelphia as a lawyer. But son Charles had invested all of his own money, as well as money belonging to his brother John Quincy, in a business that failed. He had not been able to get over feeling that he was doomed to failure, and so had begun to drink.

On 17 November 1800, thirty-two senators and one hundred six representatives met for the first time at the Capitol building. Each house had its official pen-maker, who mended and sharpened the goose quills to write with. Also

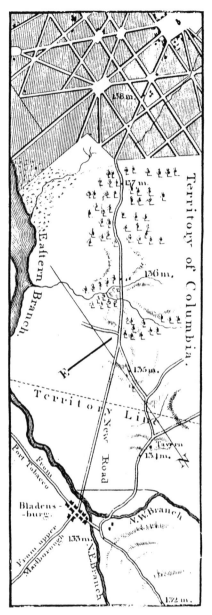

At last in 1804 a traveler was able to buy a "strip" map showing every highlight along the road from Philadelphia to Washington City. This portion shows only the last few miles of the long trip. But note the town of Bladensburg—the scene of a terrible battle only ten years later. (*The Library Company of Philadelphia*)

each house had its official sealer, whose job was to close letters and packages with official red wax seals.

But evidently many congressmen were having the same

trouble finding Washington City that John and Abigail Adams and others had. Because there were not enough members to have a quorum, the opening of Congress had to be postponed until 21 November. Three inches of snow fell the night of 20 November, and the big day was scheduled a third time.

Finally at 10:00 A.M. on 22 November, the mechanics, businessmen, military, and other professional people of the city met at the Little Hotel to form the grand procession. But the parade marshals were still squabbling over which of them was to be the grand marshal. The parade never did get started.

President John Adams arrived at the Capitol without them. He spoke to Congress assembled in the section that was completed. "I congratulate the people of the United States on the assembling of Congress at the permanent seat of their Government," he spoke as loudly as he could. "And I congratulate you gentlemen on the prospect of a residence not to be changed. Although there is cause to apprehend that accomodations are not now so complete as might be wished, yet there is great reason to believe that this inconvenience will cease with the present session."

Most of his listeners could not hear a word of the president's speech. Windows rattled and the audience shivered in the unfinished room.

The building was filled with heroes. Many veterans of the recent revolutionary war had come to work at the Congress House on Jenkins's Hill. Some had been officers, some prisoners of war; some had served while still teenagers. John Marshall, an army officer for six years, was now secretary of state but was soon to begin thirty-four years as chief justice of the Supreme Court.

With the senators sat such brave men as Thomas Jefferson (vice president), John Langdon (New Hampshire),

James Hillhouse (Connecticut), Gouverneur Morris (New York), John Armstrong (New York), Jonathan Trumbull (New Jersey), Henry Lattimer (Delaware), John Eager Howard (Maryland), Stevens T. Mason (Virginia), Wilson Cary Nicholas (Virginia), Jesse Franklin (North Carolina), Charles Pinckney (South Carolina), Jacob Read (South Carolina), Abraham Baldwin (Georgia), John Brown (Kentucky), Humphrey Marshall (Kentucky), and Joseph Anderson (Tennessee).

Other veterans that day included Theodore Sedgwick (Speaker of the House), Nathaniel Macon (North Carolina), General Thomas Sumter (South Carolina), General Peter Muhlenberg (Pennsylvania), Joseph B. Varnum (Massachusetts), John Davenport (Connecticut), Philip Van Cortlandt (New York), James Smilie (Pennsylvania), Joseph Hiester (Pennsylvania), Colonel Levin Powell (Virginia), Benjamin Taliaferro (Virginia), Robert Williams (North Carolina), Thomas Pinckney (South Carolina), Robert Goodloe Harper (South Carolina), and Matthew Lyon (Vermont).

A constant rain turned Pennsylvania Avenue into a sea of mud as the congressmen left to attend a reception at the President's House. In a day of surprises, the biggest surprise of all was finding a long line of hacks and carryalls waiting to carry them the muddy mile from the Capitol to the White House. Washington City had hardly any carriages, and this parade of covered coaches had been hired off the streets of Baltimore to come for this special occasion.

The congressmen arrived soiled and wet at the president's front door, running from the hacks across a wooden bridge into the entrance hall. Music was probably supplied by the six members of the Marine Corps Band. John and Esther Briesler, the only servants, had put a great deal of food on the table for the guests. But the guests were shocked because the two servants had not been dressed in livery, and the food was not served in the most elegant manner. The Adamses were very proper people, and their few receptions had been stiffly formal. This may have been Abigail's way of suggesting to Congress that there were not enough servants supplied to run the President's House.

The ladies of Washington and Georgetown arrived to call on Abigail Adams before she even had time to unpack her clothing. In fact, most of her clothing and personal goods had been sent from Philadelphia by ship, and like the editor Samuel Smith, her ship had not arrived. She told Nabby that she had not even a looking glass with her. And the few lamps she had carried with her did not begin to light the many rooms at night.

Nevertheless, a social call had to be returned. Even though four ladies came at the same time in one carriage to see her, a lady was expected to return a visit within a few days to the homes of each of the four. Abigail spent the better part of a day riding the three or four miles to return each visit. One day she managed to return fifteen calls all in the same day. Then she could treat herself to a day at home and write a letter to Nabby.

"The house is upon a grand and superb scale, requiring about thirty servants to attend and keep the apartments in proper order, and perform the ordinary business of the house and stable. . . . The lighting of the apartments, from the kitchen to the parlors and chambers is a tax indeed, and the fires we are obliged to keep to secure us from daily agues, is another very cheering comfort.

"To assist us in this great castle and render less attendance necessary, bells are wholly wanting, not one single one being hung through the whole house, and promises are all you can obtain. This is so great an inconvenience that I know not what to do, or how to do it."

Abigail complained very carefully to Nabby. It made no

sense to her that they should be surrounded by forests, and yet not be able to get enough wood to burn in their fireplaces. The Brieslers had not been able to find anyone to cut wood, or to cart it to the house. One man offered to bring coals, but they needed a grate to put the coal in before they could use it in a fireplace. Nowhere in the city had they found an ironmonger who could make a grate. Everyone in the city was so cold that at last the public officers had sent to Philadelphia for woodcutters and Pennsylvania wagons to carry the wood into the city.

"We have indeed come into a new country," Abigail wrote to Nabby, adding cautiously, "You must keep all this to yourself, and when asked how I like it, say that I write you the situation is beautiful, which is true. Upstairs there is the oval room which is designed for the drawing-room, and had the crimson furniture in it. It is a very handsome room now, but will be beautiful when completed."

While she was writing to Nabby, Abigail was called downstairs to see one of the servants from Mount Vernon. The widow, Martha Washington, had sent a haunch of deer meat, and Betty Lewis, George Washington's sister, had written a neighborly letter sending Mrs. Washington's love, and inviting Abigail to visit at Mount Vernon.

"Health permitting, I will go before I leave this place," Abigail wrote, when she went back upstairs.

"The house is made habitable, but there is not a single apartment finished, and all withinside except the plastering, has been done since Briesler came."

Had it not been for the Adamses' loyal servants, the Brieslers, they would have had many more discomforts. The main stairway had still not been built. No fence surrounded the president's yard. In fact there was no yard, and no shrubbery to hide what hung on the clothesline to dry. Even their underclothing hung outdoors for all the world to see. "The great unfinished Audience room [today it is the East Room] I make a drying room to hang up the clothes in."

Meanwhile, in Washington City, many new shops had now opened. Because most members of congress still powdered their hair or wore white wigs, small hairdressing shops mushroomed on Pennsylvania Avenue. Snuff and tobacco shops did a booming business. Using snuff was so much the fashion that one man in Congress had a full-time job refilling the snuff urns placed in both houses. Members from the frontier states sneered at men who used snuff. They chewed their tobacco and spat it out on the new carpet, since they saw no better place to spit.

The men who came from backwoods country to the city to represent their states had much to learn about the manners that their city-bred friends thought were important. A gentleman did not spit on the carpet or in a fireplace, but always took himself to the corner of a room to spit. Some of the men came from areas where it was common to give a handshake upon meeting. Many others recoiled from this unwanted touching, especially because so many country people had the habit of blowing their noses without benefit of handkerchiefs. A man even had to buy a pair of dance slippers if he wanted to go to the dancing assemblies held at Mr. Stille's new hotel once a month. Men wearing boots were not allowed on the dance floor.

Meanwhile, at the Capitol, business moved slowly. The Supreme Court had little to debate. They met only twice a year. Senators sat for only a few hours a day. The arguments in the House were what kept the newspaper editor busy.

What should be done about a mausoleum for George Washington? Many congressmen thought they should put up a monument and let it go at that. The seventy thousand dollars they had planned to spend would be better spent on the poor.

Then there was the problem of choosing a national emblem. A very convincing speaker stood up for the rattlesnake. "The snake was an emblem of eternity among the ancients of the old world," he argued, "and the finest emblem of the U.S. that can be found. It never acts but defensively . . . it never strikes without giving due warning, but when it does strike it is fatal."

While these debates were going on, editor Samuel Harrison Smith was having his own private battle with the Speaker of the House. He could not hear what was said, and asked if he might sit closer to the front.

The Speaker (Smith gets even with Theodore Sedgwick by not writing his name in the newspaper) refused the request. When Smith argued that he could not hear, and therefore could not tell his readers what was going on in the House, Sedgwick had the editor thrown out.

Smith, not easily discouraged, climbed up to the gallery and sat himself among the visitors. When the Speaker saw him there, he ordered the sergeant at arms to throw him out bodily.

"Whoever would overturn the liberty of the nation must begin by subduing freedom of speech!" Smith shouted in his newspaper. Smith claimed that by throwing him out of the public gallery, Sedgwick had violated his rights as a private citizen. Sedgwick complained that he did not like what the editor had written about him in the newspaper. Both men were furious, and perhaps each was testing his own powers.

At last Smith had to leave his seat. Sedgwick fired one more volley of words, saying that hereafter the clerk would send the editor the news that the House wanted the newspaper to publish. The editor was forbidden to return.

But Smith's battle for freedom of the press and the American citizen's right to know what was going on, had just begun. This sort of censored news was happening in India, where a government official erased what he did not want in print. But it was not supposed to happen in the United States. "Times are changed," Smith reported to the world in his newspaper. "But the Editor remains unshaken in his regard to truth, which shall still be spoken Whatever or Whomever it may affect."

Several congressmen jumped into the fray. A month later, members of the House of Representatives agreed that Sedgwick had "assumed a power not given him by the rules of this House" in throwing Smith out of the gallery. Later the rebuke was changed to read that the Speaker could not throw any person from the gallery when it was open, or from the lobby when that person had been introduced by a member of the House. A few days later Smith went back to his seat, and Theodore Sedgwick announced that he was going to retire.

On New Year's Day, President John Adams held the last of his levees for very important people only. Dressed in black velvet, with silver stockings and knee breeches with silver buckles, he received his guests, who stood in a circle. Each man in turn heard a few words from the president, then bowed and left. Like all of Adams's levees, the occasion was stiff and formal. Almost like an audience with a king, it was not an event that any of them enjoyed.

Everyone's attention was on a large problem that arose from the voting. On 4 December the electors had met to choose the president. They had almost no reason to expect trouble. All had gone smoothly when George Washington was elected. That time, every one of the electors had voted for the same man.

Then, at the last election, John Adams had received a majority of the votes, so again there had been no problem. This time two parties had put up candidates for the office, but the electors still expected nothing unusual.

The Federalists wanted John Adams for a second term, with Charles C. Pinckney for his vice president. A Democratic-Republican party was backing Thomas Jefferson for president, with Aaron Burr for his vice president. Just before Christmas, on 23 December, everyone knew that Adams had not been reelected.

But then who was going to be president? What could not possibly happen, had happened. Jefferson and Burr received the same number of votes from the electors.

The Constitution had said that the man who received the most votes was to be president, and the other man would be vice president. Because they both had the same number of electoral votes, the House of Representatives now had to decide which man to make president. "It is a subject of deep regret," wrote Samuel Harrison Smith, "that the Constitution of the U.S. in directing the manner in which a president and vice-president shall be chosen, has not been more explicit."

Again and again the members of the House voted and counted the votes. Every time they came out the same. Behind the scenes angry men tried to convince other angry men to vote differently. Tempers flared, and some threatened to fight. Thirty-five times the ballots came out the same. At last, on the thirty-sixth try, some men who had voted for Burr were persuaded to change their minds. They would not actually vote *for* Jefferson, they said, but they did agree to turn in a blank vote. Inauguration Day was only a few weeks ahead when Thomas Jefferson finally learned that he had been elected president and Aaron Burr vice president.

6

Thomas Jefferson's City

"Usually changes in a government are marked by villainy and bloodshed."
                              —Margaret Bayard Smith in 1801

The owners of Conrad and McMunn's tavern were having trouble attracting customers to the houses of entertainment they had recently opened about two hundred paces from the Congress House. One house was just for boarders who came and stayed a long time. The other, less elegant, was for stage passengers and travelers. The stable was large enough to hold sixty horses. But so many taverns and boardinghouses had sprung up in Washington City that Conrad and McMunn were beside themselves trying to fill all their rooms. Until they were saved by a pig.

Early in February, a country farmer wandered into town with a pig that he had taught some tricks. The tavernkeepers immediately put up a sign advertising THE LEARNED PIG, and paid for a large ad in the city newspaper. Five times a day, except on Sunday, the farmer showed customers all the

Conrad & M' Munn

HAVE opened houſes of entertainment in the range of buildings formerly occupied by Mr. Law, about two hundred paces from the Capitol, in New Jerſey avenue, leading from thence to the Eaſtern Branch. They are ſpacious and convenient, one of which is deſigned for ſtage paſſengers and travellers, the o her for the accommodation of boarders. There is ſtableage ſufficient for 60 horſes——They hope to merit public patronage.

City of Waſhingron, Nov. 24, 1800.   tf

Conrad and McMunn placed this advertisement in the Washington City newspaper just a few months before the "Learned Pig" arrived to stay awhile. (*Library of Congress*)

pig's tricks, at a cost of fifty cents for an adult and twenty-five cents for each child. The price was high, but the show brought the crowds.

To the audiences (most of whom could not read or write themselves), the pig seemed to actually read printing as well as writing. The farmer claimed that his pig could spell, and tell the time of day using any man's watch. To the amazement of those watching, the pig seemed also to add, subtract, multiply, divide, distinguish colors, and even tell how many people were present.

"Draw a card from the pack," read the newspaper advertisement, "keep it concealed, and the pig will discover it."

The pig stayed only until 12 February. The House of Representatives had just begun casting their ballots to decide whether Jefferson or Burr was to become the next president. Everyone expected that important decision to be announced at any moment, and the business of the new government could begin.

Thomas Jefferson moved into the rooms that he had been keeping at Conrad and McMunn's tavern about the time that the pig moved out. Jefferson's bedroom there had a small adjoining parlor. But in many ways Jefferson surprised people even more than the Learned Pig had.

He did not arrive in royal style with a host of servants or hide himself from the public. He walked alone or with his friends around the city, wearing his plain suit of homespun material. He horrified some people by shaking hands with every man—even some who might not be classed as gentlemen. And in a most unkinglike manner, he ate a public dinner—sitting in the eating room with the rest of the boarders!

By the time the final ballot was cast, and Jefferson was sure that he was to be the next president, only two weeks were left before the inaugural to choose the men he wanted in his cabinet. John and Abigail Adams had not yet moved out of the President's House. And in case anyone was planning a large parade or inaugural celebration of any sort in Washington City, that person had only a short time to plan it before the big day of Wednesday, 4 March 1801.

Across the country, almost everyone welcomed Thomas Jefferson with open arms, especially because he was not of the Federalist party, which had run the country for the past twelve years. The people had had enough of men in government who reminded them of the old royal behavior they recalled from the days before the Revolution.

In Boston, the inaugural edition of the *Columbian Centinel* put a black border around this article, as if someone very important had just died:

YESTERDAY EXPIRED
Deeply regretted by MILLIONS of grateful Americans
And by all GOOD MEN
the FEDERAL ADMINISTRATION
of the
GOVERNMENT of the United States

Animated by
A WASHINGTON, an ADAMS:—a HAMILTON,
KNOX,
PICKERING, WOLCOTT, M'HENRY, MARSHALL,
STODDERT AND DEXTER

Age 12 years

Philadelphians planned one of their super-size parades for which they were becoming famous. Many officials in that city had not given up hoping that Philadelphia might still become the nation's capital again. For the parade, each state had its own float, pulled by high-stepping horses, and carrying young people all dressed in white. The largest float had an elegant ship of state, called the *Thomas Jefferson*, and was drawn by sixteen horses.

In Washington City, however, there was no parade at all. At daybreak on Wednesday, 4 March, James Hoban's Washington Artillery Company made certain that no one could sleep late and miss the events of this special day. The company fired off a series of loud volleys from their muskets.

Before daybreak, President John Adams left town in his

own plain carriage. Behind him, in the president's stables, he had left seven horses, two carriages, and the silver-mounted harness. They were to be sold because Adams's enemies said he had paid for them with money that should have been spent on furniture.

Crowds of people who lived in all the surrounding communities poured into the wide city streets to see some of the excitement. They could not witness the actual swearing-in of the new president, because no building was nearly large enough to hold them. But just being near those who did take part in the coming ceremonies was enough to satisfy them.

At 10:00 A.M. the Alexandria Company of riflemen arrived in front of Conrad and McMunn's tavern, along with the Washington Artillery Company. They paraded in front for two hours, waiting for the new president to appear.

About noon, Thomas Jefferson strolled out of the tavern with a group of friends and walked casually up New Jersey Avenue toward the Congress House. He was dressed plainly—much too plainly to suit Thomas Carpenter and Charles Varden, tailors who had just opened their shop on Capitol Hill and planned to get rich making elegant uniforms and clothing for congressmen and their wives. As Jefferson entered the Capitol, the artillery fired another volley.

The Senate chamber was packed with bodies. Never had so many crowded into the building. Jefferson sat down, and as soon as the audience was silent, he arose and gave his inaugural address in a voice so low that few people noticed he had a slight stutter.

He was tall and thin, a little round-shouldered. But his gray eyes gave him a friendly look. He had come alone to Washington City. His beloved wife had died nineteen years before, leaving him to raise two young daughters without a

In a rare moment, Thomas Jefferson dressed in his best for this portrait painted by Rembrandt Peale. (*Library of Congress*)

mother. Now his two married daughters, Martha Randolph and Maria Eppes, were both expecting babies and had stayed at home in Virginia.

Margaret Bayard Smith, the wife of the newspaper editor, had managed to get one of the seats in the Senate building. She remarked later in her diary that "usually changes in a government are marked by villainy and blood-shed." She was thrilled that "in this our happy country," the change could take place with no disorder at all.

After he spoke, Jefferson walked over to the clerk's table and took the oath of office before Chief Justice John Marshall. The new president then walked back to his rooms at the tavern, in the company of his staff.

If the people who had come to see the excitement were disappointed that there was no parade or that Jefferson did not even ride in a fancy carriage, they did not let it bother them. They knew that Thomas Jefferson believed strongly in equality—and that he was showing them that even the president was no different from other men. The visitors to the city celebrated by themselves. At night the city was illuminated brilliantly with candles flickering in every window of every house. To people who had never seen a street lit up at night, the effect was dazzling.

One night Jefferson attended a dinner for forty men at the Eagle Tavern. And on Saturday, 14 March, the largest party was held at Gadsby's Hotel in Alexandria. That night all thirty-two of the hotel's front windows were lit by candles.

Jefferson stayed at Conrad and McMunn's for two more weeks. The house on Pennsylvania Avenue was still far from comfortable, and he wanted some changes made. First, he ordered the bells installed that the Adamses had never managed to get. Next he wanted the main stairway built up to the second floor. The builders took another two years to finish the stairway, but at least Jefferson made them begin the work.

The new president also wanted the room where Adams had held his formal levees changed into an office. His entertaining, when he got around to it, was to be very informal.

He had the front door moved to the north side of the house (where it is today). Then he changed what had once been the entrance hall into a sitting room, and put in windows where the front door had once been. Jefferson had it painted blue, and it has been known as the Blue Room ever since.

But the most immediate change was tearing down the wooden "necessary out offices" that Mr. Thornton had been told to build outside the President's House, not even hidden from public view. Every house in America, including the president's, had to have a necessary. But Jefferson had seen something better on his travels.

He had two modern "water closets" installed upstairs. Water closets were a new idea. A reservoir of water above them flushed out waste "at command." This may have been the water system that Lewis Beebe had described the year before. If so, it may not have been in working order until Jefferson had it completed.

Very few homes in America had water that could be pumped indoors into a tin basin in the kitchen. Most city people sent their servants with buckets to the nearest pump in the city streets. Only in Philadelphia was there a reservoir, "the ninth wonder of the modern world," with wooden pipes that carried water from the river to pumps near city houses. Here in Washington City, servants had to carry their buckets far from home to pump drinking and cooking water for the family.

The new capital city shared one problem with all the other cities in the country—sicknesses that no one could explain, although Adams and many others had their own theories. In the winter, people had the "flux." In the summer they had the "ague." In the late summer, just when the dangerous season should be over, came the yellow fever. Doctors had not yet heard of germs, and most medical men had decided the cause of sicknesses was the smells or "emanations" that came from the earth or swamps.

"It's because they took down so many trees," said some people, "and so spoiled the natural air conditioning." But just as many others believed the opposite—that if the trees were cut down, and the sun allowed to shine on their house roof all day, they would have no illness.

No one seemed to suspect that the water they were drinking caused much of their illness. Dr. Benjamin Rush of Philadelphia said that people who drank coffee and tea all the time did not get sick with dysentery, a disease that killed many people. But he and other physicians gave the credit to the powers of tea and coffee. They never realized that tea and coffee drinkers were unwittingly saving themselves because they boiled their water to make their hot drinks. Boiling water killed many of the germs that might have killed them.

A Washington City bookstore sold Noah Webster's book, *Epidemic and Pestilential Diseases*. Webster, who knew nothing at all about diseases, said that typhoid fever came from the air. Especially from air that smelled bad. Meanwhile sewage was leaking into people's water supplies, night soil from chamber pots was buried in the soil to make vegetables grow larger, and whole families died of typhoid and other fevers without ever knowing why.

When yellow fever raged in the cities, all the blame was put on the ships that had recently anchored in the harbor. People thought the ships brought the fever from foreign lands. Sometimes they blamed the bananas that came in the ships, simply because bananas were the same color as the people who had the fever. No one noticed that the water barrels on the ships' decks were a breeding ground for mosquitoes.

Dr. Rush spent many years trying to find a way to cure yellow fever. He often mentioned the "moschetoes" he saw when the fever was at its worst, but he never made the connection between yellow fever and the annoying little pests that buzzed around the swamp water. No one noticed that when a mosquito drew blood from a person with yellow fever, it then carried the disease on to the next person.

August and September were the "bilious months" in Washington City. Only the bravest and hardiest people remained then to see what diseases might come from the "pestilential emanations" that arose from the tidewater swamps. At daybreak, people saw the mist rising from the water and smelled its foul odor. They covered their noses and mouths with a handkerchief and hurried along to higher ground. Members of Congress stayed safely in their own states during those months. Capital city people with friends in other cities packed their clothing and made long visits. The poor, who had nowhere else to go, counted on homemade medicine and charms to keep them safe.

In 1801 Thomas Jefferson was no exception. He spent only a few months in the President's House, then he took off for Monticello. "I consider it as a trying experiment for a person from the mountains to pass the two bilious months on the tide-water," he said. "I have not done it these forty years and nothing should induce me to do it." So saying, he made arrangements for riders to carry messages to him at Monticello. In only two days he could receive information and important papers a hundred miles away, and in less than a week, the rider would return with his answer.

Besides, both of his daughters were to have babies during the summer, and he intended to be there. Martha Jefferson Randolph, his eldest, had already had five healthy children, when her daughter Virginia was born that summer. But

Jefferson was worried about his youngest daughter, Maria Jefferson Eppes. Her baby, Francis Eppes, was delicate and did not live long. In spite of stories and rumors to the contrary, neither baby was born at the White House.

The City Gets a Mayor

"Went to a shop in New Jersey Avenue to look for black chintz. A poor little store—there are too few inhabitants for any business to be carried on extensively."
—Mrs. William Thornton in 1800

For years the three commissioners had dreamed that one day Congress might take over running the capital city. By 1801 the city and county of Washington had outgrown the three men who had struggled to manage its affairs.

The city had never had any money. If the United States had been a kingdom, people complained, Washington would have been the residence of nobility and so become wealthy. Much of the land was government-owned, so it was free from taxation. Most of the people who lived in Washington were only temporary residents. They paid taxes in other states that they considered their "real homes." That left fewer than four hundred people who lived in the city and actually paid taxes there.

In addition, the city was too underdeveloped to attract large businesses and industries that might have paid taxes.

Mr. Piercy had just built an excellent sugar refining house that could be seen for miles down the Potomac because it was eight stories high. But the few factories that had begun in Washington seemed to last only a short while. Another sugar refinery owned by Thomas Law had closed after only four years.

Now the city faced a problem. Congress, in creating the federal city in 1790, had not been clear about how it should be governed or how its bills should be paid. Local residents discovered that many in Congress believed they should not have their own locally elected government. After much debate Congress agreed to give Washington City its own local government. In 1802 the president appointed Robert Brent the city's first mayor. He was reappointed every year until 1812, when the elected city councils began to select the mayor. The new government had two chambers of councilmen, much like a miniature national government. The councilmen were elected by the 325 property owners who had lived twelve months in their electoral district and had paid their taxes.

The council rented a house on Twelfth Street from the building company for $200 a year, bought a supply of writing paper, firewood, and candles, and began thinking up ways to pay for their extravagances. Not until seventy-five years later would the federal government help pay the city's expenses. The councilmen, like those in other cities, had to find other means to get money.

The heavy traffic gave them their first idea. From now on, district citizens must pay taxes for their wheels—$12 a year for each chariot, but less for owners of phaetons, carriages, chairs, sulkeys, and down to only $2 for a wooden two-wheeler. A peddler had to pay $16 to do business in the district, while tavern owners forked over $10 for the privilege of selling wine, and another $15 if they "kept a billiard table for gain."

The new mayor had other money-making ideas for the city, but he had to limit himself to those that cost nothing and yet brought in cash, like holding fairs on the Mall in May and November, and talking the citizens into opening a market. When a mad dog was killed near the jailhouse, the council decided to tax dogs.

When citizens complained that they missed all the cultural advantages they had enjoyed when they lived in Philadelphia, Mayor Brent encouraged his friends to start subscribing to the Columbian library (started earlier in Georgetown) for fifteen dollars a year. Then he headed a group to begin building a theater at fifty dollars a share. Unfortunately the first theater groups that came to town put on such stupid plays that the theater was many years getting finished.

The mayor installed oil lamps on some of the main avenues of the city for dark nights, paying a lamplighter one hundred dollars a year to light them at sundown with just enough oil in them to keep flickering until after midnight. Until now, late meetings had to be scheduled for nights when the moon was full so people could find their way home. One stormy night, Dr. Thornton told his wife he could not have made it home if it had not been for the brilliant flashes of lightning.

The new lanterns were a huge improvement, but the town boys could not resist aiming stones at the glass lamp globes. The lamplighter refused to pay for the broken globes. Mayor Brent hired a policeman. His pay was two hundred dollars a year plus all the fines he could collect. During his rounds of visiting every part of the city at least once a month, the policeman earned his living by collecting fines. He got

Another early 1800s view of the young city from across the Potomac, showing the busy waterfront and, in silhouette, the half-finished Capitol on Jenkins's Hill (*The National Archives*)

ten dollars for every water-filled hole in a yard that had no fence around it, and the same if he caught a homeowner snitching the gravel and sand that the city had spread on the streets to pave them.

By November 1802 Pennsylvania Avenue was "paved" from the President's House to the Capitol, with earth, stones, gravel, and sand. The new Washington Hotel boasted a footwalk from its door all the way to the Capitol for walkers.

In only two years, the city population doubled in size to almost four thousand people. Traffic now was hopelessly snarled. Everyone who could possibly afford to attach two wheels to a horse had some sort of vehicle. Many of the streets were too narrow for two wagons to pass. And in the wider avenues, carriages, wagons, six-horse coaches, peddlers' carts, and riders on horseback charged wildly up and down either side of the road they pleased, crisscrossing and running head-on into each other.

The mayor began widening streets, and passed a new law that forced vehicles to drive on the right-hand side of the street. Now the policeman had to move fast in order to collect the one-dollar fine from every carriage driver who continued to drive on the wrong side of the street. In 1803 Congress extended the city charter for fifteen years and gave the city the power to establish schools and get more money from taxing.

That summer was extremely hot, with not a drop of rain for forty days. All the kitchen gardens in the city wilted. The newspaper editor put his new Fahrenheit thermometer under a black hat and said it registered 101 degrees. Under a white hat it was two degrees cooler. Sales of white and light colored hats doubled.

Folks who could afford it took their families to Andrew Villard's "Little Cottage" for sweet cakes, macaroons, oysters, and, on special days—ice cream. Because ice cream could not be kept cold, Villard made it only on Wednesdays and Sundays in the summer, and sold it for twenty cents a glass.

In July, one brave man started "a hazardous experiment." Unable to bear the heat another day, he waded out into the Potomac. People were terrified of plunging their hot bodies into cool water. Who knew what might happen? The old people around warned that such nonsense had been known to cause instant death.

But the unnamed man had not gone into the river without taking precautions. First he drank a glass of water "to cool down his body" for the shock ahead. Then, at 10:00 P.M. on a hot night, he waded into the river, stayed only fifteen minutes, dried off with warm towels, and immediately jumped into his warm bed "with a view to prevent my taking cold," he explained. Three days later he tried it again, staying a half hour. Still he did not drop dead. By August he was going in every two days. For timid swimmers, an inventor advertised his new "nautical machine" to save persons from drowning. The "machine" was a belt of cork to be fastened around the waist.

Brent knew the long drought meant fires in the city. The "fireproof" city was still filled with many wooden structures, even though notices had been put in the paper by the president and commissioners that the wooden shacks had to go. Now a recent fire had destroyed public records at the Treasury Department. Another burned down the Washington Academy, leaving only its bare walls. The mayor ordered every homeowner to buy a leather fire bucket and keep it near his front door.

At the cry of "Fire!" every man grabbed the nearest bucket and raced with it to the source of water. Women and children formed lines to pass the empty buckets toward the water. The men lined up opposite them to pass the heavy filled buckets up to the fire fighters. Citizens in each ward formed their own fire-fighting companies. The city had bought new fire ladders to help them reach roofs. After a fire was put out, each man searched for the buckets with his name painted on the side, and took them home again.

Most fires began in chimneys because they were full of grease from cooking. Often they flamed up without warning. By law, each homeowner also kept a pound of brimstone where someone could throw it instantly onto a chimney fire. The brimstone made clouds of stinking vapor that choked off a small, beginning fire.

Eventually the mayor had to clamp down on greasy chimneys. He ordered every homeowner to have his chimney

The city was growing so fast that in May 1804 a city census showed there were now more than 4,000 living there, including 717 slaves and 228 free blacks. The professions listed in 1804 included:

4 architects	19 printers
2 merchant taylors	82 laborers
1 notary public	18 bricklayers
50 clerks	1 turner
21 merchants	2 sailmakers
16 stonecutters	1 cooper
2 lumber merchants	1 nail cutter
18 carters	13 house carpenters
17 taylors	2 linners
15 gentlemen	1 painter & carpenter
1 glassman	23 shoemakers
2 nailers	3 pumpmakers
8 butchers	1 millwright
8 watermen	9 tavernkeepers
4 painters	13 plasterers
2 painters & glaziers	6 bakers
63 carpenters	1 carver & gilder
12 joiners	1 brickmaker & layer
6 physicians	1 gunmaker
7 cabinetmakers	7 stonemasons

swept every three months between April and October, and every two months in the winter. The chimney sweep arrived sometime between five and seven in the morning. No matter how carefully the housekeeper tried to cover up the fireplace opening, the sweep's vigorous strokes sent soot flying out into every room of the house. For all the sweep's hard work,

2 booksellers	1 huckster
1 shoe merchant	2 grocers
24 officers of government	2 ditchers
6 constables	1 brewer
4 hack drivers	4 lawyers
2 measurers	1 well digger
2 pedlars	8 blacksmiths
1 composition maker	2 masons
1 billiard table keeper	1 watchmaker
2 saddlers	2 hairdressers
1 conveyancer	3 ministers of Gospel
5 schoolmasters	1 woodsawyer
8 messengers of Depart-	6 brickmakers
ments	1 collier
9 hatters	1 dentist
1 upholsterer	1 scower
3 ropemakers	33 shopkeepers
2 gardeners	7 ship carpenters
1 wood measurer	1 fisherman
1 ship joiner	1 wheelwright
2 chairmakers	1 post man
1 glazier	1 harnessmaker
2 coachmakers	117 professions not desig-
1 jailer	nated

he earned only ten cents for cleaning a one-story chimney; double that for a two-story job. In addition, if a chimney should catch fire within two months after being cleaned, the sweep had to pay five dollars to the homeowner.

When they were sure the summer's heat had ended and cool weather returned, the congressmen filed back into the city, gladdening the hearts of tailors, boardinghouse keepers, dancing schoolmasters, and hundreds of shopkeepers. The senators, now all wearing the new-style top hats, met in their wing of the Capitol. They were more or less content with their meeting place. After all, being cold in winter and having the roof leak during rainstorms was nothing new to these men. Stoves were being installed under the floor to make the winter more bearable.

In a vaulted room in the basement, the Supreme Court met. They were a distinguished group, with Justice John Marshall as their chief. A judge—who sat with Marshall for many years—said Marshall was a tall, plain man, whose clothing looked as if it had been made for someone else and bought in a secondhand store. But Marshall had a hearty laugh, great patience, and a superior mind that allowed him to sweep away what was not important and get straight to the heart of a matter. He was the perfect choice of a man to establish the power of the Supreme Court.

With Marshall were other men of equal patriotism. Justice Samuel Chase had signed the Declaration of Independence as a member of the Continental Congress twenty-five years before. Justice William Cushing had watched his father preside over the trial of British soldiers after the Boston Massacre. Justice Alfred Moore had been a captain of dragoons during the Revolution. Justice William Paterson had also been in the Continental Congress and was once the governor of New Jersey. Justice Bushrod Washington was a nephew of George Washington. Taking their seats temporarily in the basement room of the Capitol building, these men might have been shaken had they known the Supreme Court was to meet for the next sixty years in the same room.

The most important project during Jefferson's first summer in office was to find space for the House of Representatives. They also wore top hats during working hours, making it even harder for a congressman in back to see all the way to the front rows. In the south wing, where the House chamber was supposed to meet some day in the dim future, workmen put up a temporary low brick building. It was to be torn down later, after walls and a ceiling were built around and over top of it. The men called it "the Oven," and they meant no compliments.

The already erected cellar masonry of the south wing was in such bad shape that it had to be taken down all the way to the foundation and begun again. One of the problems with finishing the chamber for the House had been its size. How many men were going to be using it? Since the 1800 census had been counted, it appeared that many more people were now living in the United States than anyone had supposed. And that meant more representatives for them would be showing up after the next election. More chairs in the chamber, more rooms at boardinghouses, more families coming to the city, more places for them to eat.

Eating a public dinner, once a rare occurrence, now became common in Washington City because so many men had left their wives back home and had no one to cook for them. A popular place to eat was William Tonkin's Beefsteak and Oyster House on Capitol Hill, where many of the patrons of Blodget's Hotel went to eat. Seamstresses, also, found much work to do for the men living alone. Sewing was one of the few ways that a single woman or poor widow could earn money respectably.

The mayor had been only a short time in office before the complaints began coming in. Some complained that the police officer was doing nothing for his pay. Others complained about the great danger from leaking and unstable ferryboats. Some of the ferries were no more than two canoes with boards across. To reach the town of Alexandria and travel to southern states from the capital city, a traveler either had to detour many miles north to where he could cross the Potomac River safely on Chain Bridge or else use the unsafe private ferryboats. The mail coach was too valuable to be trusted to a rickety ferry. Somehow an iron bridge had to be built across the Potomac. But until it could be done, the mayor ordered that all boats used as ferries must pass a careful inspection.

The city council, still looking for ways to make money, added taxes on slaves and personal property, even taxing clothing and workmen's tools. But there was still not enough money to open schools. Donations for a school came from many people, including Thomas Jefferson. The city opened two schools—the Eastern school near the Capitol, about where the Library of Congress stands today, and the Western school near the President's House. Although many private schools were near the city, no school until now would take poor white children whose families could not pay. Now even poor boys had the chance (providing their families did not need to send them to work) to learn reading, writing, grammar, and arithmetic, for free. Paying pupils, at the same school, also learned geography and Latin for their five dollars each quarter.

Black children, those whose parents were free blacks, had no school until 1807. That year three black men (who could not read themselves) determined that their children would have their own school. They built a small frame schoolhouse near the Navy Yard, and hired a white teacher. They had come from slavery, and there were still many slaves in the city, but at least after 1 January 1808 no more slaves were supposed to be imported from other countries.

Mr. White was the principal teacher of the Western

school, and his wife agreed to teach a few selected girls at the school. The Reverend Robert Elliot was principal of the Eastern school. Each man received five hundred dollars a year, which sounded like high pay until they learned they also had to rent a schoolhouse, buy the wood for heating the school, and pay other incidental expenses, such as the wages of the assistant teachers. The children went to school every day except Sunday and had a bit more than a month off in summer. Once a year the children had to stand for oral exams, usually held at one of the hotels. Everyone in town came to hear how much the children had learned.

The capital city now had much to brag about in its newspaper. It had its own militia, uniformed in dark blue coats with white vest, breeches, stockings, and round black hats. A turnpike road now ran from Georgetown to the Capitol, built of earth and brick, and covered with gravel— and far more comfortable for carriages than other roads that were built of hard stones.

A huge dock was being built at the Navy Yard. The Marine Barracks there was a mass of brick buildings, two stories high, and the Marine Warehouse was three stories high. Unfortunately, President Jefferson had just cut down the Marine Corps to four hundred men and cut the navy in half, from forty-two vessels to only twenty.

Changes and Surprises in the City

"Higgledypiggledy, or the one nearest the door gets the best seat."

—Anonymous in 1803

Thomas Jefferson was a surprise. Although no one in America knew exactly how a president ought to behave, the two presidents the citizens had already voted into office were very alike. Both had been very proper and careful of every move they made. Jefferson was much more relaxed.

In his first speech to Congress, he announced that wars seemed to be over. Peace had been made with the Indian nations. Only one villain still had to be dealt with, and the president thought that would be simple enough. The ruler of Tripoli had captured some American ships in the Mediterranean Sea and was holding the crew and passengers hostage until the government paid huge ransoms for their release. Two months later, the Pasha of Tripoli declared war on America. Jefferson sent a naval squadron to deal with the situation quickly.

The new president often rode around Washington on horseback. He used the fancy carriage only when his daughters came to visit. At night he slept alone and unattended in one of the many second-floor rooms.

Jefferson did not schedule appointments with people who wanted to see him. He got up at dawn and went to bed at ten. In between, anyone could knock at his door and ask to speak to the president. Naturally this meant (to Jefferson, anyway) that the visitor must accept him the way he was. If he was slopping around the house in old slippers and a favorite loose-fitting shirt, he made no attempt to dress up. This informality caused a good many funny stories to circulate around town.

A New Hampshire senator said he once found the president "dressed better than usual one morning." He was wearing an old coat, worn down to the threads, a vest, corduroy pants, and clean stockings, although his shirt was dirty. One writer said it was because he was a Virginian.

"Virginians have some pride in appearing in simple habiliments [clothing], and are willing to rest their claim to attention upon their force of mind and suavity of manners."

Whatever the cause for Jefferson's love of comfortable old clothes, Americans were quite used to hearing the stories about their informal president. But the stories had not reached the other side of the Atlantic when the British sent a new ambassador to Washington City. The ambassador, Anthony Merry, had already lost much of his dignity being seasick on a stormy sea crossing from England. Merry and his wife had hoped to leave the miserable ship at the first port, which was Norfolk, and travel the rest of the way by highway. But there was no road from that city to the capital. The winds blew hard out of the west and the ship struggled for six days longer up the Potomac River. The unhappy

Merrys were the first off when it reached Alexandria. From there they managed to hire an uncomfortable coachee, bounding over roads so full of holes and stumps that they were both certain they had arrived in a country filled with barbarians. After finding a "hovel" where they could stay until they found a suitable house, Merry began recovering his composure. He dressed early in the morning, in full uniform, complete with sash and medals, and called on President Jefferson.

The "Envoy Extraordinary and Minister Plenipotentiary of His Brittanic Majesty" could at first hardly believe his eyes. In Merry's own words, he was "introduced to a man as the President of the United States, not merely in an undress [which to him meant Jefferson was not dressed in a matter befitting such an important occasion] but actually standing in slippers down at the heels, and pantaloons, coat, and underclothes" [shirt] that even looked soiled.

The more Merry thought about it, the madder he got. By the time the interview was finished, Merry was sure that the president had actually studied the situation and then had dressed in that fashion for the sole purpose of insulting the king of England.

Not even an invitation to dinner improved Merry's opinion of Jefferson. Any congressman could have told Merry what to expect at Jefferson's dinners, but apparently no one did.

Dinner was served at 3:30 P.M. The guests usually stayed until six, but all were to be gone by eight. Everything about dinner shocked Merry. No preference at all was given to the important guests. The president had offered his arm to the lady who acted as his hostess (sometimes it was Dolley Madison, or one of Jefferson's own daughters), and led her into the dining room. Mrs. Merry had expected to be escorted in to dinner on the president's arm herself, as one of her rank would have been back home in England. However, the pair were left to find their own way to the table. Higgledy-piggledy, or "the one nearest the door gets the best seat," was the order of seating in Washington City.

Jefferson held his first "open house" at noon on 4 July. The grounds were open to everyone, but only one hundred were invited into the dining room to nibble at the goodies carried up from the kitchen by Jefferson's house slaves. The other visitors had just as good a time staring goggle-eyed at a group of Cherokee chiefs (the first Native Americans that many Washington people had ever seen) and listening to the marine band.

So many Americans felt close to the president that presents began to arrive at his house by the dozens. Many were Indian artifacts—peace pipes, wampum, feather head-dresses. Jefferson's father had once been an Indian trader, and many gifts had been sent by Native American friends whom the president had known since his boyhood. Jefferson put them all on display in the front hall of the President's House.

Farmers often saved their prize products to send to the president. One farmer sent the hindquarter of the largest calf anyone had ever seen. It had already begun to decay. A town in Massachusetts, famous for its cheese-making, sent a huge cheese that weighed over a ton and was made from the milk of nine hundred cows. Jefferson shared it with the visitors who came to his New Year's Day open house, until the smell of it drove them all out into the open air.

Usually the New Year's open house was presided over by one of the president's daughters. Martha and Maria came to Washington City for a visit about November and returned to Virginia early in January. Martha was not yet thirty.

Maria lived only until 1804, dying when she was just twenty-six. The sisters loved the excitement of tea parties and shopping in the city, and both of their husbands were active in politics.

While they were in the city, Jefferson's daughters usually attended the church services held by the chaplain at the Capitol. Most churches had no building of their own until 1806. What continually surprised visitors from other countries was the variety of different religions, all getting along with each other.

Many small businesses in the city were doing well. But because Jefferson was a widower, and there was no full-time hostess to greet people, the social season was not what it might have been. And because of that, men's and ladies' tailors, food catering businesses, fancy dress shops, and some others were suffering.

Business perked up when Dolley Madison, wife of Secretary of State James Madison, helped to enliven the dragging social scene. She had parties and started a few fashions of her own. Dolley was partial to turban-type head coverings, which she topped off with ostrich or egret plumes, and started a demand for fashion that the shopkeepers were only too happy to encourage. Dolley often acted as hostess for Jefferson at the President's House. She was an unusually friendly and warm lady, loved by many of Washington's citizens.

In the city's younger days, the young people of Washington had often held small parties of their own. When they could find someone to play the fiddle, they danced until the small hours of morning. "The young people danced until one of the Violin strings broke," Anna Maria Thornton had written in 1801.

But now Washington had large hotels with space for big

Evening Dresses in Jan.y 1809

From the pages of *Portfolio* magazine, two ladies show that in 1809 the closer the waistline was to the shoulders, the more fashionable a dress for the evening. (*The American Philosophical Society*)

parties. Hotel proprietors often held public balls. Then when it became evident that few people in the isolated village of Washington knew the latest dance steps from the large cities of the country, the same hotels held "Practice Balls," complete with French dancing instructors.

Ladies, eager for invitations to the small affairs at the White House, hopped from one fad to another trying to outdo their rivals. Silk shawls, turban wigs, soft velvet dresses, *bafta* from India, all had their turn. Then from France came the idea of wearing a flower in one's hair—but such a flower! It began the evening as a rose bud. Then as a high point came in the dance, the young lady touched a small spring beside the bud and presto, a full crown of roses appeared around her curls. With another touch of the spring, the crown turned back into a single rose. The effect must have been enough to cause a heavy drinker to swear off liquor—at least for the evening.

Jefferson did not like to eat dinner alone. Almost every day he invited a dozen guests. His food was excellent, cooked by a French chef. The president wasted no time in the old custom of drinking toasts. His guests chatted freely, simply enjoying each other's company. At these occasions, just as at his larger dinners, there was no lining up for important guests to enter the room first. The president, himself, with the hostess of the evening on his arm, was always the last to walk into the room. Meanwhile, his grocery bills rose steadily, using up a great deal of the president's own money. Only his steward worried, saying that it often cost fifty dollars a day to feed the president's many guests.

The city had now planted Lombardy poplar trees along Pennsylvania Avenue, from the President's House to the Capitol. When vandals chopped several down one spring night, Mayor Brent had them replaced and also replaced the city's one policeman with two. The four rows of trees on either side of the gravel carriage road were for more than just beauty. According to the newspaper, they were placed there to attract lightning because they were higher than the houses. The poplars had been Jefferson's suggestion, and he probably was angered at what the newspapers said. "I really look with commiseration over the great body of my fellow citizens, who, reading newspapers, live and die in the belief that they have known something of what has been passing in the world in their time," Jefferson wrote to a Virginia friend, who had asked his advice on starting a newspaper. Then he added, ". . . the man who never looks into a newspaper is better informed than he who reads them."

Jefferson had a large library of his own books, and he encouraged Congress to give a thousand dollars a year to build up the Library of Congress collection that had begun many years earlier. Already it was the finest library in the country. The city had a few small private library companies, but membership in them cost fifteen dollars a year, and the poor were not welcome to join. In the poorer district by the Navy Yard there was a book-buying club. Through the club, a poor family could actually own a book for eighty-seven cents. The favorite book of the year was Parson Weems's *Private Life of George Washington,* with its now-famous, concocted story of young George chopping down the cherry tree.

From May to November, the marine band played on Saturdays outside the President's House, until the president could stand the tinny racket no longer. He had an "Italian band" imported from Italy, and so it became fashionable to have an Italian band at parties.

Several artists now lived in the city. The most famous of them was Gilbert Stuart. One year the president had a

Looking down Pennsylvania Avenue toward the White House from the Capitol Hill. Washingtonians admired the Lombardy poplars planted by Thomas Jefferson not only for their

portrait painted of each of the visiting Indian chiefs. The Native Americans often came to the city to attend the New Year extravaganzas.

One year the celebration included a concert with a display of grand fireworks, featuring "the Battle of Butterflies" and a splendid sun of various colors with a bright revolving flower in the center. This was followed by "a grand Indian

beauty but because they were taller than the houses and therefore provided homeowners safety from lightning strikes. (*The National Archives*)

dance given by a party of savages of the Missouri nation lately arrived in this city."

City people who liked action better than art, music, or fireworks, had the racing season to look forward to. The Jockey Club held races every fall in a field north of the city. Every business closed, and the entire city went off to the races.

Dr. William Thornton, who now was head of the U.S.

Patent Office, had so many inventions stored away that he had to move to larger quarters. The new nation needed all the inventors that could be found. When a person invented something he thought worthwhile, he sent a model of it to the patent office. The model was stored by Dr. Thornton, who also saw to it that each inventor received a patent explaining his invention in detail. Jefferson bought one invention, called a polygraph, made by Charles Willson Peale, a famous artist. With the polygraph, a person could write a letter while at the same time two other pens automatically made copies.

In 1804 Baron Alexander von Humboldt brightened the social scene. He was handsome and exciting, and made a very good reason for a round of parties in what might have been a dull social season in the capital. A great geographer, Humboldt had been exploring the Amazon and Orinoco rivers in South America.

"We have lately had a great treat in the company of a charming Prussian baron," Dolley Madison wrote on one occasion. "All the ladies say they are in love with him. . . . He is the most polite, modest, well informed, and interesting traveler we have ever met, and is much pleased with America."

One night Jefferson entertained Jerome Bonaparte and his bride, the former Elizabeth Patterson. Jerome, the youngest brother of Napoléon, had fallen in love with the American girl, but his brother had insisted he come back to France and marry into royalty. Jefferson tried to tell Napoléon that Jerome had married into a very fine family, but the French leader was consumed with the idea of making himself an emperor. An American sister-in-law was not welcome in his family. Napoléon had his brother's happy marriage annulled.

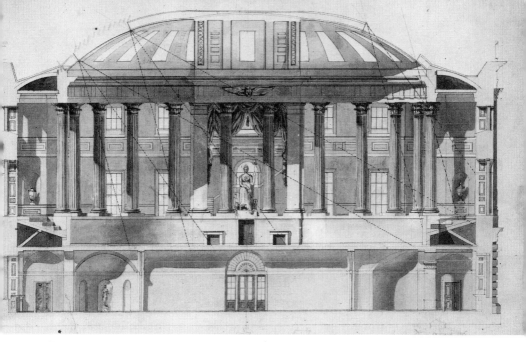

Benjamin Latrobe's plan for finishing the House of Representatives included corn tassels at the tops of the columns. (*Library of Congress*)

Benjamin H. Latrobe was now the surveyor of public buildings, a misleading title, because he was the architect hired to complete all those jobs that had not yet been done. He finished the president's main stairway and stopped his roof leaks. He made the senators happy by stopping the leaks in the north wing of the Capitol building, also. Then he began to raise the walls of the south wing around "The Oven" where the representatives met.

To put the finishing touches on the Capitol building, two Italian artists, Giuseppe Franzoni and Giovanni Andrei, came to do the stonework. They carved fluted columns, designed by Latrobe, and at the top of the columns, where columns always had acanthus leaves, they carved corn tassels instead—a truly American symbol. "These . . . ," said Latrobe, referring to the corn tassels, "obtained me more applause from members of Congress than all the works of magnitude or difficulty that surrounded them."

The most surprising event of Jefferson's presidency was

the Louisiana Territory purchase, an event that had people arguing from all sides. To Jefferson, it was a large amount of land won without a war. But some people said the land was worthless, that Bonaparte was pretty smart to make the United States pay for the land he probably would have thrown away anyhow. Many people were angry because they thought their land in the east would no longer be valuable now that so much more land was available. The discovery that the new land west of the Mississippi River was probably as large as all the land east of the river came as a great shock.

President Jefferson had sent his secretary, Meriwether Lewis, and a soldier, William Clark, with a party of men to see just what really was out there. Slowly word filtered back to Washington City—along with some of the wonders that the party had captured in the wilderness beyond the river.

Everyone in Washington City saw the trophies Lewis and Clark sent back because Jefferson proudly displayed them all. Once cages of grizzly bears stood out on the lawn for all to see. The White House collection included chunks of salt from a "salt mountain" near New Orleans, a "wild dog of the prairies," and a cage marked "four magpies." Not knowing much about the habits of magpies, Lewis had no way of knowing that by the time the cage arrived, one of the magpies had put an end to the other three.

The capital city had grown up and become beautiful in the eight years that Jefferson was president. Many streets were "paved" with earth, sand, and gravel. Mud slowly had given way to flowers and plantings. Orchards had gradually become small parks.

Only one sight disgraced the city streets. Strangers from other countries brought it to the attention of the city dwellers who had grown so used to the scene that they no longer thought of it. "Why," people asked continually, "in a country known now all over the world for liberty and independence, were there men in chains and being driven through the city streets to be sold?"

Some people, especially Quakers, had already freed their slaves and sent them to Ohio or other northern states where they would be safe. Meanwhile some slaves who hired out to work in the city were allowed to keep some of their wages and were eventually able to buy their freedom.

In 1805 a congressman introduced a resolution that all slaves in the district should be freed as soon as they reached maturity. But other congressmen argued that no trained laborers could be found except slaves and free blacks. The resolution was defeated.

A five-dollar fine was charged for any slave caught on the streets of Washington City after 10:00 P.M. Slaves were also fined five dollars if they made any noise or disturbance, quarreled, played any games of chance, danced, or were caught drinking. The fine could be paid by the master. But he didn't have to pay the fine. The master could pay fifty cents instead and have the slave whipped and sent home. Washington's black population had grown so fast that in 1808 the lives of all African Americans were regulated and restricted by the "black code," a collection of laws passed by the city council. Starting in 1812 every free black person had to register and carry at all times a paper proving his or her freedom.

During much of Jefferson's presidency, Britain and France had been at war. Both countries had shown little respect for the flag and ships of the young United States, stealing their cargoes and capturing their seamen. At last Jefferson ordered no more trade with the warring countries.

This embargo only hurt the Americans, and it was repealed when Jefferson left office.

When asked what he intended to do next, as he packed up to go home to Monticello, Jefferson answered, "I shall retire to my family, my books, and farms. And having gained the harbor myself, I shall look on my friends still buffeting the storm with anxiety indeed, but not with envy. Nature intended me for the tranquil pursuits of science."

With him went one of the largest private collections of natural history and Native American artifacts in the country, including fossil bones, a buffalo head, moose and elk antlers, Indian relics, and one heavy package that was stolen from the ship before reaching Monticello. The thief who took it, evidently disappointed at what he found inside, threw the contents into the river. Except for a few pages that floated ashore and were found in the mud, the Indian vocabulary collection that Jefferson had worked on for eight years was lost forever.

The City of James and Dolley Madison

"The Directors and citizens went over the Washington Bridge . . . and all had a frugal repast. . . ."
—*National Intelligencer and Washington Advertiser*, 1809

James Madison was short and tended to get lost in a crowd. But Dolley, his wife, was always nearby. And because the tall plumes in her headdress waved high above the tallest men, the Madisons were easy to spot.

At daybreak on Inauguration Day, Saturday, 4 March 1809, a salute of cannons from the Navy Yard and a nearby fort shook sleeping citizens from their beds. The city was so filled with people from states near and far that any person who expected to have a seat in the House chamber had not a moment to lose. Masters sent servants to the Capitol at once to save seats for them, and the chamber was overflowing several hours before noon. More than ten thousand people crowded along Pennsylvania Avenue and the streets around the Capitol.

Congressmen arrived at the House of Representatives'

James Madison, with his wife, Dolley, brought refreshing changes to the capital city. (*Library of Congress*)

chamber at eleven. When all the important department heads had been seated, Thomas Jefferson sat on the platform. Because no speech was required of him, he could enjoy the occasion. Outside, the shouting and clapping grew louder as James Madison, escorted by troops of cavalry, arrived. Chief Justice Marshall administered the oath, and Madison gave his inaugural address. Then the cavalry fired two rounds from each of their "minute guns," small cannons that fired once every minute; they were usually used to signal emergencies or some great event. Outside once again, the new president reviewed nine volunteer militia companies.

That evening four hundred people—including Thomas Jefferson, who did not leave the city until the next morning—thronged the inaugural ball at Long's Hotel. The newspaper editor, who was there with his fun-loving wife, claimed it was the most brilliant and crowded ball ever known in the city.

Even though the assemblage was packed with ladies and foreign dignitaries dressed in their most glittering outfits, no one missed the fact that President Madison was wearing a full suit of cloth manufactured completely in America. Nor did anyone miss what Dolley was wearing. Her gown was buff-colored velvet; her neck and arms swathed in pearls. On her head she wore a sultan's turban from Paris with plumes donated unwillingly from a bird of paradise. Dolley had once been married to a sober Quaker who died, leaving her a very young widow. People who had known her then, in her Quaker gray dress and bonnet designed to hide a woman's face, would hardly have recognized her now.

Hundreds more stood outside on the street to hear the music and catch a glimpse of the dancers. Much of the capital city's gaiety has always centered around the famous people who have gone there to work at running the government. Even the poorest Washington citizen could look on the important people as his neighbors. Dolley Madison's warmth and friendliness encouraged this sense of community.

Because there was much to celebrate, other cities held

inaugural balls and parades of their own. The United States had doubled in land size and had increased by almost two million people, in just the past eight years. Washingtonians enjoyed hearing about the festivities in other cities. Such stories in the local newspaper helped bind the growing nation together.

Right now Washington's citizens were worried by talk of war. They looked at the ships in their own Navy Yard and were anxious about how small the American navy had become. Only the frigates *Constellation* and *Congress* were there—both out of the water being repaired. And the army too had grown smaller during the Jefferson years.

The editor of the Washington newspaper worried too. He saw that the principal royal actors in Europe were almost all young, vigorous, and dangerous leaders. Although King George III of England was almost seventy-two years old and not likely to start a war, the editor was not so sure about the others. The Grand Sultan of the Barbary States was a cruel man, and the United States was still paying money to keep him from taking Americans hostage. And then there were the others.

"Francis II, Emperor of Germany and King of Austria, was 42 last February," he wrote in the newspaper. "Napoleon I, Emperor of France, will be 41 next August. Frederick William III, King of Prussia, will be 40 next August. Alexander I, Emperor of Russia, was 33 last December. We have no data to judge the age of the present Grand Sultan who it would appear is likely to take a pretty active part in the contest."

For several years now, British ship captains had been stopping American ships and taking off men, even young boys, claiming they were "British subjects." Two boys even had been kidnapped from a small boat that was taking them across Chesapeake Bay to their school.

When Madison became president, the frigate *Constellation* was in the capital city being repaired at the Navy Yard. (*U.S. Naval Institute, Annapolis, Md.*)

Everyone was relieved when Congress decided it was time to build up the United States Navy. Its largest warships were frigates with from twenty to forty-four guns. They were three-masted and swift on the ocean, but clumsy in the rivers. Besides, each needed a crew of over two hundred men to manage the huge square canvas sails and heavy oiled ropes. The United States had eight frigates in March 1809, but only two of them, the *Constitution* and the *Chesapeake*, were "officered, manned, victualled [provided with food], and ready for service," according to the Washington newspaper.

Brigs, more easily maneuvered than frigates, needed smaller crews. But the navy now had only five, only one of which was in Washington, the *Nautilus*. The navy had two schooners, but they were both in Norfolk, "nearly ready for service." A third frigate, the *Boston*, was in Washington but "in need of repairs," said the newspaper. In actuality, it was so badly damaged that the repairs never were made.

The rest of the U.S. Navy was scattered from Boston to New Orleans.

★ ★ ★ ★ ★ ★ ★ ★ ★ ★ ★ ★ ★ ★ ★ ★ ★

The U.S. Navy in March 1809

FRIGATES

Constitution. Commodore Rodgers. 44 guns. In New York.
"Officered, manned, victualled, ready for service."
(This is the ship later known as Old Ironsides and is today at the Boston Navy Yard.)

United States. Captain Stephen Decatur. In Norfolk, Virginia.
"Almost ready to sail."
(This ship was captured by the British in October 1812.)

Essex. Captain Smith. 32 guns. In Norfolk, Virginia.
"Almost ready to sail."
(This ship was captured in March 1814; sank in a tornado, July 1814.)

Chesapeake. Captain Isaac Hull. In Boston.
"Officered, manned, victualled, ready for service."
(This ship had been damaged in a battle off Norfolk in June 1807. Captured by the British in June 1813.)

President. Captain Bainbridge.
"Will be ready to sail by July."
(This ship survived the War of 1812.)

Congress. At the Navy Yard in Washington.
"Needs repairs."
(This ship survived the War of 1812.)

Constellation. At the Navy Yard in Washington.
"Needs repairs."
(This ship survived the War of 1812 and can be seen today in Baltimore Harbor.)

Boston. 28 guns. At the Navy Yard in Washington.
"Needs repairs."
(This ship was finally found beyond repair and on 24 August 1814 was still at the Navy Yard. She was burned to prevent the British from taking her.)

CORVETTES
John Adams. Captain Evans. Baltimore.
"Being repaired."

SHIPS:
Wasp. Captain Robinson. In Norfolk.

BRIGS:
Hornet. Captain Dent. In New Orleans.
Argus. Lieutenant Jones. Gone to France.
Siren. Captain Gordon. In Baltimore and Charleston.
Vixen. Lieutenant Dent. In New York and Charleston.
Nautilus. In Washington, "preparing for service."

AND 2 SCHOONERS, 1 CUTTER, and 172 small GUNBOATS spread all over U.S. waters.

The U.S. Army in 1809, under the direction of Brigadier Generals James Wilkinson, Wade Hampton, and Peter Gansevoort, also needed to be modernized. It consisted of regiments of Artillerists, Light Artillery, Light Dragoons, Infantry, Riflemen, and Surgeons. Among the younger officers were such names as Lieutenant James J. Bowie of the Light Dragoons, Major Zebulon Pike of the Infantry, and Lieutenant Zachary Taylor of the Seventh Infantry, who

Looking across the Anacostia River, also called the eastern branch of the Potomac, to the Navy Yard as it appeared about 1810 (*The National Archives*)

was to become president of the United States forty years later.

Outfitting an army was not cheap. Muskets with bayonets cost $11. Pistols for the cavalry, carrying a musket cartridge, cost $8. A sword was $6, and another $3 for the iron scabbard. Rifles, the newest army weapon and much more accurate than muskets, cost over $16.

While Washington City people worried about possible war, they also had many distractions. One was the new Washington Bridge that crossed the Potomac River. The road from Washington City to Alexandria was a tortuous twelve-mile route, connecting to a ferry that was dangerous after heavy rain and sometimes could not be used at all. Because the mail route went to Alexandria, something had to be done.

All winter the newspaper had reported the progress of

the new Washington Bridge, often calling for more timber or for carpenters. The weather was the coldest in twenty years, with ice nine inches thick. What might happen when it melted? Would ice chunks coming down the Potomac crush the bridge before there was even a chance to try it? Everyone breathed a sigh of relief on the day the ice finally melted without sweeping the bridge along with it.

At last, on Monday, 17 April 1809, the longest bridge in the United States, and probably in the world, said the paper, opened for the directors and citizens to walk to the other side. The money for building had almost run out, so the builders had to limit the celebration to making "several appropriate toasts" and eating a frugal meal, before they walked back to the city again. One month later, the completed bridge opened to carriages that traveled on the new stone-and-gravel turnpike road between Washington City and Alexandria.

Called the Long Bridge, it was almost a mile long and was located where the Fourteenth Street Bridge is today. Three carriages could ride beside each other and still leave a passageway, separated from the roadway by a railing, for foot passengers. Twenty lamps lit it at night. Two draws, one thirty-five feet wide and the other narrower, opened "by the most ingenious machinery that could be worked by a boy of ten years," for ships to pass through.

New houses of entertainment, on the other side of the bridge, now opened for Washington City people. Less than a mile from the bridge, a place called Sebastian Springs enticed ladies to come for public dinners and tea parties. The owner had hired a waiter who could play the violin, and furnished private rooms for ladies. He also advertised that "Ladies can be supplied with Syllabub Under the Cow every morning until six and every evening until 7 o'clock." Whipped syllabub was a popular drink, made by mixing sugar, lemons, an orange, white wine, and rich cream. To make it "Under the Cow," the chef put everything in the bowl first, then added milk all frothy and straight from the cow into the bowl.

The new bridge also made it easier to go to the Arlington Sheep Shearing every 30 May, with a stop at Sebastian Springs for a barbecued prize-lamb dinner. Visitors from several states entered the contests at Arlington, all of them geared to turn the United States into producers of wool, especially now that no patriotic American was buying wool from England.

The prizes were big money to country people. The finest ram won a silver cup, or $60, for its owner. The best American-born sheep shearer took home a prize of $5. The woman who wove the best five yards of cloth mixed with silk won $15—but the silk she used in it had to be taken from old worn-out silk clothing. Americans could not afford to throw anything away.

Now that trade was cut off from England and France so much of the time, Americans had to make products for themselves that they once bought from Europe, and to come up with new ideas. Dr. Thornton, head of the U.S. Patent Office, encouraged clever people by giving them patents on their inventions. Luckily many inventive brains seemed to be working on this side of the Atlantic Ocean.

One man invented an instrument called a pencil, which wrote with powdered lead. The first woman to receive a patent was Mary Kies of Connecticut, who discovered a way to weave straw with silk or thread. Another man invented a "pigeonhole mailbox" for a tavernkeeper whose inn had become the local post office. Each hole had a glass window at one end, much like the mailboxes inside post offices today.

One inventor suggested a new use for cement, called stucco. "It won't catch fire if your neighbor's house burns," he explained. But housebuilders soon discovered they could use it to build houses with poor wood, like gum or willow, that could not last through changes in the weather. Covered over with stucco, the poor wood lasted longer.

John Baxter patented a spinning and weaving machine that every family could afford. A girl of thirteen, named Charlotte Mills, said that she spun more than one hundred balls of flax yarn in only fourteen hours using Baxter's machine. Every thrifty family grew flax, spun it into linen yarn, and wove their own material to make sheets, pillowcases, blankets, shirts, and dress material.

Ladies bought the new metal pens invented by Mr. Peregrine Williamson, and sent off invitations to parties and other entertainment.

Now that Washington City had a president's wife who loved going to parties and the theater, some of the cultural treats that people had enjoyed when Philadelphia was the capital city came to the federal city. A National Museum and Portrait Gallery was almost completed, and the city was full of famous artists. A popular fad now was to schedule sittings with one of the portrait painters. Several sittings were needed to do a single portrait, but the artist was able to make other copies after the first portrait was completed.

Music did not fare as well as art. Since Jefferson's Italian band left, the Marine Corps Band was the only group that claimed to play music. Most people had never even heard of an orchestra. For dancing assemblies and private parties, four musicians supplied all the music needed. New the summer of 1809 was "Mrs. Madison's Waltz," but the most fashionable songs of the year were "Sigh Not for Love" and "The Bird upon the Summer Spray."

Stage actors found a good living in the city, where eager audiences paid one dollar to sit in a box, separated from the ordinary people who had paid seventy-five cents to sit in the pit. Plays rarely made more than two appearances, because the playgoers wanted three or four different plays in a week. None of the plays were great literature. Actors had no time in between plays to learn lines. After the "writer" had decided on a plot, the actors made up the words as they went along.

Each play had two names, in case the first had not explained what it was about. One night's entertainment was usually two very different plays, with comic songs and dances during the intermission. Sometimes the entertainment was musical, but what audiences liked best were comedies. The jokes were usually about the latest political news. One night, when the newspaper was full of stories about the British navy taking sailors off American ships, the audience was in hysterics watching *John Bull: An Englishman's Fireside*. Another night the performance was *The School for Reform, or How to Rule a Husband,* plus a comic opera called *The Rival Soldiers, or Sprigs of Laurel.* A special show for the Fourth of July was *The Point of Honor, or The School for Soldiers,* to which was added an entertainment called *The Independence of Columbia.*

Not everyone in the city could afford to be entertained, however. The city had built a poorhouse at Sixth and M streets. When it was full, the city paid two dollars a week to board a poor family in any boardinghouse that would take them. Then the city built an almshouse in the country, where the poor could live and make articles to sell for the city's benefit.

A girl named Sarah Rogers boarded with Mr. Underwood. Sarah had been born without the use of her arms or legs, yet she could paint flowers and landscapes, mix colors, write her name, thread a needle, and cut paper—using only her mouth. Mrs. Underwood invited the public to see her perform, every day from nine in the morning to nine at night. Her audience paid twenty-four cents each. Mrs. Underwood pocketed the money.

Rosanna, a teenage black girl, had run away from her mistress in Alexandria and was put in the Washington City jail. She was five feet tall, with a large scar under her right jaw. Rosanna had a blue striped jacket, a light colored dress, old stockings, and a pair of new shoes. The newspaper said that her owner must come, pay the costs of keeping her in jail, and take her away. If the owner did not show up, Rosanna was going to be sold "for her jail fees and other expenses."

Within a few years, the situation grew even worse for black people. Every free black person had to carry a certificate that proved he was free. If the paper was lost or taken from him, he was put in jail as a runaway and could be sold back into slavery. Only if a white person came to the jail to prove that that black was free, and paid the cost of the jail expenses, could the black be set free once again. Most cities had similar "black code" laws.

In May, a young Quaker hardware merchant from Philadelphia named Abel Satterthwaite arrived in the capital city to see how his money was being spent. He was engaged to be married in a few months to Susanna Claypoole, the daughter of Betsy Ross. The stagecoach carrying Abel passed through the town of Bladensburg, crossed the eastern branch of the Potomac River, and rumbled through a forest."When coming out of the woods, we had the pleasure of seeing the CAPITOL," Abel wrote in his diary. But thrifty Abel had heard of the high prices in the capital city, and was taking no chances. He rode on through the city and ate his lunch in Georgetown. Then he took a stagecoach for 112½ cents to Alexandria where he spent the night with friends at no cost.

"Crossed the celebrated bridge over the Potomac," he wrote. "A large frame structure, and if it does but stand, a great improvement to that part of the country. Nearly one mile long and of a good width, but if there is much current in the river, I think it will not stand long. Toll high, one dollar for a carriage and two horses.

"The keeper of the Alexandria Stage office told me he paid 1,000 dollars per year for the Stages' crossing. About four miles further crossed another large bridge and cause-way, made over an arm of the river, which extends but a little way. The turnpike is a pleasant road to travel, being made of gravel, and not so much used as to be cut up much."

The next day, Abel went back to Washington City and began acting like a tourist. He stayed the night with friends opposite the famous Seven Buildings. Forty or fifty houses, according to Abel, and a market house, had now grown up around the President's House.

"The President's House, or rather palace, is a large build-ing, built of white stone and surrounded by a wall about eight feet high. . . . The Capitol, as it is called, consists of two large square buildings which are intended at some future day to be joined together, making one large and grand de-pository for the collected wisdom of the Nation to be placed in several months of the year. And I think if they had much wisdom, they could manifest it in another way much more to the advantage of the nation and their own credit than they do in squandering hundreds of thousands of public money on such useless, uncomfortable buildings as the Cap-itol & the palace is, in my view."

The east front of the President's House after the north and south porticos were added (*The National Archives*)

Having unleashed his fury at "expending the hard earnings of his fellow citizens in pompous show without substance," the young Quaker walked on to the Navy Yard. But here he was even more disturbed, because he saw "so many men employed in preparing the works of destruction and death."

"A little eastward of the Capitol, near the Navy Yard . . . there is the most of a town of any part of the City, as it is called, being perhaps 200 houses, built pretty much together. . . . There appears to be but very little improvement going on in the city, except the Canal, which I think will cost much more than it will be worth."

Abel left Washington at five the next morning. Late that night when he stopped in Baltimore, he found a letter waiting for him at the mail coach tavern from his beloved Susanna, which put him in much better humor.

Finally in 1812 the Capitol at the end of Pennsylvania Avenue has two matching buildings, although the passageway between them was built only of rough wood. (*National Archives*)

By early June 1812 every American, white as well as black, began to worry about losing his freedom. Talk of war was no longer just rumor. President Madison's attempts to stop the British from looting American ships had succeeded no better than those of Thomas Jefferson. Now British ships had managed to blockade most of the important ports so that no ships could either enter or leave the country. Merchants had to stop doing business. To add to the nation's problems, stories and tales arrived every day in the capital city from westerners who complained that the British were encouraging the Indians to rise up against them.

Communication was poor between Washington and the

western states, but between Washington and the enemies overseas any attempt at communicating was hopeless. Word traveled so slowly from one side of the Atlantic to the other that, when the British decided to back off and stop the blockades on 17 June 1812 the message arrived months later. Meanwhile on 18 June in Washington City, Congress voted to declare war.

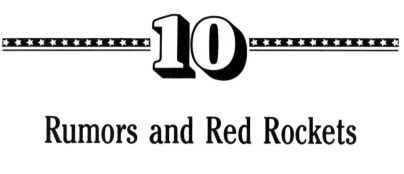

10

Rumors and Red Rockets

"I therefore keep the old Tunisia sabre within reach."
—Dolley Madison, 1813

Every able-bodied white male in the Washington District between eighteen and forty-five years old reported for service in the militia. Not even government clerks were exempt. Older men signed up to work in volunteer companies to defend the homefront. Mayor James Blake of the city appointed some of these older men to patrol the streets at night. Newly appointed officers went off to borrow a book, or buy one like *The Handbook for Cavalry Tactics* that was now on sale at the local bookstore. The drafted younger men marched off to learn how battles were supposed to be fought.

At Greenleaf Point and the Navy Yard, men built earthworks strong enough to support heavy guns. But it took time to make a supply of cannons and cannonballs. Until there were enough cannons, some of the rivers in the east had to make use of "Quaker guns," like those on the Delaware River. A Quaker gun was a straight tree trunk, painted black, and placed at such an angle that it looked like a cannon pointed toward ships coming upstream.

The secretaries of war and of the navy advertised to local butchers and tradesmen that they were receiving proposals for shipments of beef and clothing for the growing army and navy. Supply wagons had "U.S." painted on their sides. Soon the letters were appearing everywhere. A New York man patented his "durable knapsacks with 'U.S.' " stamped on them, and asked the officers of different volunteer companies to adopt them for all their men. Before long people joked that the letters stood for "Uncle Sam."

Many businessmen lost their trade. Because of the continuing blockades, no one could import goods. Some tried smuggling foreign-made goods into the country. But by December 1812, the blockade by British ships made even smuggling impossible. Besides, Americans had suddenly decided it was unpatriotic to want goods made by other countries. Some, like Romulus Riggs of Georgetown, who imported goods from England, simply closed their businesses. Others advertised in the paper to get rid of their imported merchandise as soon as possible. Crates of French bonnets and yards of British woolens sold quickly.

The panicky preparations for war did not last long. All the battles were miles away from the capital city. When people in the city read the newspapers they learned only what had happened ten days earlier.

The war near the Canadian border went very badly that summer. First the United States forces surrendered a fort between Lake Huron and Lake Michigan. This gave the native chief Tecumseh a chance to line up all the Northwest Indian tribes on the British side. Then the Americans, led by General William Hull, retreated from Canada to the fort in Detroit, because Hull thought the Indians might cut his supply line. In the middle of August the Indians massacred the Americans at Fort Dearborn after promising them they could leave the fort safely. The next day, General Hull surrendered Detroit without firing a single shot. He was court-martialed later for cowardice, and only his record as a brave soldier during the Revolution saved him from being executed.

"Our troops were much disheartened at this period by the very disgraceful surrender which had been made by General Hull of his troops at Detroit," wrote one young army lieutenant in early September, as his detachment rode to the Canadian border.

The Americans might have won a great victory at Niagara, but the militiamen from New York refused to follow their commanders out of their own state and over into Canada. The men claimed that state militia were supposed to stay in their own state. Their officers could not force them to move on, because even they had to admit that the rules had not been set down clearly. Some states had even refused to form state militias.

Luckily, the British aim was none too good. One young soldier explains why in his diary. "The British always aim too high," he wrote with his own unique spelling, "in consequence of their cartridges being so heavy that no man dare lay the but of his musket to his sholder, or if he does do it once he will not like very well to try it again, and consequently he will hold his musket in such a way as not to nook the sholder of himself. He will put the but down along his side under his arm, and in this case the musket, when the holder thinks his piece is level, will always be elevated."

Before long the "summer soldiers" began to desert. The Washington newspaper printed detailed descriptions of each deserter. President Madison threatened, and then promised forgiveness to every deserter who went back to his company within three months.

War was usually put on hold during the rainy and winter seasons, anyway. Neither army could push cannons through mud, and neither navy could go far when the lakes and rivers froze over. Three months was time enough to get the deserters back in line, and meanwhile the young United States had much to do to prepare for the battles that would come the next spring.

After thirty years of peace, the treasury had no money set aside for war. The arsenals were empty and the forts in ruin. Many of the old navy ships, sold years before, still had not been replaced. The "army" was made up of raw recruits, like Lieutenant Isaac Roach. Roach had been raised on his father's patriotic stories about the Revolution, and now signed up to do his duty. When he reported for duty, he found his colonel "sitting crosslegged, reading the words of command from a book he had compiled from the French." His regiment's horses had been bought from farmers nearby, and had been "sold by their owners NOT for their many good qualities."

The provisions were impossible. The stockings, said Roach, "would fit any size foot, for if they were too short, the soldier only had to push his toes between the threads." Roach's general was so angry about the blankets supplied to his army that, according to Roach, the general "folded one up, very neatly, in an envelope, and sent it to the War Department to shew in a stronger manner than language could, the covering about four foot by three, intended for a Canadian winter." As for the soldiers' pay, Lieutenant Roach said that a "Mr. Aiken" was the only paymaster for the men on the Canadian border, and Aiken had no money at all.

The British had less success when they fought the Americans on water, and Washington newspaper readers found some heroes to worship. Captain Isaac Hull, in the frigate *Constitution*, defeated the British frigate *Guerrière*. In another battle, the guns of the *Constitution*, this time under Captain William Bainbridge, riddled the hull of another British frigate. The Americans fondly called their ship Old Ironsides after that day. Captain Stephen Decatur, on the frigate *United States*, captured a British frigate and took it back to New London, Connecticut, as a prize.

Back in Washington City the first year of the war passed without too much worry for the local citizens. In October the entire city, black and white alike, turned out for the Jockey Club Races. Courts closed. Even Congress emptied out. The ladies rode out to the track in their carriages, hampers of picnic food tucked in by their feet. Their drivers pulled the carriages up to the oval so they had an unobstructed view. The gentlemen circulated around the coaches, placing bets and viewing the ladies. People with lower social standing stood inside the oval, running to and fro for a better view as the horses rounded the track.

On 1 January 1813 the Madisons held the usual New Year's open house. Dolley wore a pink satin robe trimmed with ermine. Around her waist she wore a gold chain, and gold bracelets jangled on her wrists. Tall white ostrich plumes on her white satin and velvet turban bobbed every time she moved her head. A lady who attended the party described Dolley's dress. Then she added that the president, as usual, looked "like a schoolmaster dressed up for a funeral."

Madison had been elected for a second term. A shy man, he rarely showed his sense of humor to anyone but his closest friends. While everyone seemed to become friends with Dolley immediately, most people found Madison standoffish and cool. It took a near disaster before the people of Washington discovered the real James Madison.

The excitement and balls of the inaugural season were barely over before the British opened the war again. This time the enemy moved closer to Washington City. While some British warships harrassed American towns near the ocean ports, British Rear Admiral Sir George Cockburn, with his seventy-four-gun flagship *Albion* had orders to discover ways to capture some of the largest and most important cities—Philadelphia, Baltimore, Annapolis, and the new capital city of Washington. Philadelphia he found far up a river that was easily entered through Delaware Bay. The other three were on rivers that Cockburn's ships entered from Chesapeake Bay. One small village, he found, had only a small ferry connecting the main highway between the capital city and the large eastern cities. He added Havre de Grace, Maryland, to his list of targets.

Cockburn (he pronounced it "Co-burn") began by hitting all the small villages downstream from the larger cities that he might need to capture. Often he seemed to have uncanny skill in locating villages that were unarmed, but people reading the Washington and other local newspapers knew where he found much of his information. Citizens constantly wrote letters to newspaper editors—who published them—demanding that someone either come to protect them or send guns as "there is only one old flintlock" in their entire village.

By midsummer every port along the eastern seacoast was blocked by British ships whose captains used the same techniques perfected by Cockburn. Without being able to use its ports for business, the U.S. government was dangerously close to running out of money.

Rumors flew faster than bullets. One day a Washington

newspaper reported that some Americans had poisoned bottles of whiskey and left them where the British raiders would be sure to find them. That gave everyone a good laugh. The next newspaper told of reports that the British had poisoned the water in an American well. That was not so funny. The newspaper editor printed every rumor he heard. He had no time to check rumors for truth. Later, if he discovered a rumor was unfounded, he told his readers.

"For the last week," Dolley Madison wrote in a letter dated May 1813, "all the city and Georgetown (except the Cabinet) have expected a visit from the enemy, and were not lacking in their expressions of terror and reproach. We are making considerable efforts for defense. The Fort is being repaired, and five hundred militia, with perhaps as many regulars, are to be stationed on the Green near the windmill. The twenty tents already look well in my eyes, who have always been an advocate for fighting when assailed—though a Quaker. I therefore keep the old Tunisia sabre within reach."

Those people in the capital city who had the means to flee began packing immediately, rented their houses, and left town. Some, like the Thorntons, moved out to their country homes. Those who could not leave the capital often read the newspaper with fear and trembling. Almost every village up and down the rivers along Chesapeake Bay had its own story. Sometimes the British burned homes to the ground. At other times the raiding parties were strangely polite as they pillaged and burned public buildings.

When the Washington newspaper reported that the militia from Havre de Grace had come to protect the capital city, the citizens breathed a sigh of relief. Almost at once, Cockburn's men attacked the town of Havre de Grace to cripple the highway between Philadelphia and Washington.

When Dolley Madison sat for James Peale to paint her "miniature," she was already fond of tall hats. (*Library of Congress*)

The townspeople there were the first Americans to see Cockburn's merciless new weapon—the fiery rocket invented by Sir William Congreve. A projectile with an iron head that exploded on contact, it struck terror in the helpless wives, children, and old men who were the only inhabitants left in Havre de Grace. Filled with fire-making material, it could burn down a house. Filled with grapeshot, it exploded and could injure or kill several people at one shot.

After Cockburn showed off his new weapon and burned down several homes, he stole a new sofa to use in his ship's cabin and helped himself to a handsome thousand-dollar coach. He promised to ride the coach through the streets of Washington. And he sent word that soon he would make his bow in Dolley Madison's drawing room.

All summer, the admiral kept up his war of nerves against the people of the capital city. Sometimes he would start up the Potomac River toward the capital, sending watchful scouts off to the city with the alarm, only to turn his ships about after dark and sail back downstream. Again, he would disappear up a river across Chesapeake Bay. Once his ships arrived after dark at the small shipbuilding town of St. Michael's on the Eastern Shore. The villagers all lit their lanterns after dark—but they hung them in the trees. The British aimed toward the lanterns and shelled what they thought were houses. Up another river, the Admiral spared an old widow's house when she begged him to let it stand, and burned down another one instead.

That summer, President Madison had a serious case of "Potomac fever." The doctor told Dolley that only good nursing could keep him alive, and she hardly left his bedside for weeks. He was still sick in July 1813 when he placed General John Armstrong, the Secretary of War, and General William Winder, in charge of defending the capital city.

Washingtonians felt safer with two generals in charge, but had they known more about this pair, they would have been better off to pack their belongings and head for the hills. Armstrong had been a young man when he fought during the Revolution more than thirty years before. In the past year, he had taken a small and undistinguished part in the disastrous military events along the Canadian border. Winder was a lawyer from Maryland, with almost no military experience at all. He had managed to get himself captured near the border of Canada, and had been a prisoner of war for a while in Quebec.

The local militia did nothing to make the capital's citizens feel secure. One man, who had been watching the militia drilling, was so upset he wrote a letter to the newspaper. "They don't march straight," he wrote. "If, after a few evolutions, a solitary noncom officer is at his proper post, it is a wonderful circumstance! . . . In wheeling, they often mistake the right and left forward, and in backward wheeling it is a miracle if they are ever right."

The crisis in 1813 passed before the unmilitary soldiers learned to wheel and march in a straight line. Cockburn continued his war of nerves, this time sailing far up the Potomac River. Then, just before he reached the capital city, his ships turned back once again. His fleet, in a very nasty mood, sailed southward to Norfolk and Hampton in Virginia, where they attacked the villagers fiercely. Then, with winter approaching, they sailed for Bermuda.

Washington breathed easy once again. Parties and dancing assemblies started in the ballrooms of every large hotel. People talked of the theater companies coming for the winter season, and of the lottery to collect money for George Washington's monument, which had not yet been started. Ladies ordered the new-style dresses that clung close to the body. Even Mrs. Madison's Wednesday afternoon get-togethers began again.

Across the square from the President's House stood the new Washington Hotel. It had four dining rooms and two kitchens, a good cellar, billiard room, and thirty-five lodging rooms. Unlike smaller hotels, this one also had an icehouse, milk house, coal house, stable, carriage house, and a separate house for the owner. But what attracted customers to it was the two "bath rooms," where anyone might bathe alone for fifty cents, or three people for a dollar.

The city also had a public bathhouse where anyone who could afford the ten-dollar season ticket could bathe in warm or cold water. The manager assured his customers that warm baths actually prevented sickness and cured rheumatic complaints. The rich city people had often gone in the summer to Berkeley Springs, Virginia, to bathe in the healthful waters. Now they might bathe at home. One of the newest patents was for a portable bathtub. Its inventor even produced letters from hospitals to prove it was healthful, and from a minister to prove there was nothing immoral about bathing. A portable tub could be bought for fifteen dollars. But the habits of a lifetime cannot be changed overnight. Most people agreed it was best not to open the pores by taking a bath between September and the Fourth of July.

In Philadelphia's navy yard, workers were building a new frigate that had been baptized by a lightning strike, surely a good omen. In Boston's navy yard, another new ship, the *Independence* with seventy-four guns, was finally launched after several tries and killing one workman, a bad omen. But far from discouraging her launchers, the newspaper said, "She is not easily to be moved and will never bow to the thunder of the enemy."

But not all Americans were so confident. The wars had ended in Europe, releasing thousands of British soldiers to fight in America. The year 1814 could be the worst yet.

The Enemy Creeps Closer

"The British would never be so mad as to make an attempt on Washington."
> —General John Armstrong, secretary of war, 1814

"The Americans may cashier Madison and follow the example of France . . . and return to the protection of their former Sovereign." So claimed one European newspaper, stirring up a storm of angry protests in America.

In April 1814 Napoléon had abdicated. The French sent him to the island of Elba and put a king, Louis XVIII, on the throne. Now that the British were no longer fighting the French, many people thought the British would now try to take back their lost American colony.

Feelings were already running high against the British when the people of Washington read in their newspaper that spies often visited local taverns and carried back news to the British commanders. One ship had stopped a packet boat on Chesapeake Bay and removed from it one hundred suits of U.S. uniforms—clothing that could easily disguise any man who spoke English. Nor could Americans uncover a spy just because he spoke with a British accent. In these early days of the new country, most Americans of British descent still spoke with an accent.

The people of Washington City began to panic after rumors made the rounds that the British had now placed General Robert Ross, a professional soldier, in charge of ten thousand seasoned troops—and they were now on their way across the Atlantic. Letters swamped the newspaper office with suggestions of how General Winder ought to be protecting the capital city. He could at least plant torpedoes in the Potomac River to keep Cockburn's ships from getting as close as they had the previous summer. The only person not worried about the war seemed to be General Winder himself.

Winder claimed he had fortified old Fort Warburton (later called Fort Washington) some miles down the Potomac River from Alexandria. He said no British ship could get past that fort. And in case the British tried to come up the Patuxent River to strike at Washington, Commodore Joshua Barney was ready to greet them with his great flotilla of ships. Winder still had the militia camped on the hill (now called Observatory Hill) within sight of the President's House. Another thousand men had camped about fifteen miles from the city at a place called Woodyard in Maryland. From that point, Winder said, his soldiers could reach either the Potomac or the Patuxent river in about two hours.

The secretary of war, John Armstrong, saw no reason why the British would want to take Washington City anyway. It had no strategic importance. Surely, he said, they would much prefer to take Baltimore or Philadelphia instead.

"The British," said Armstrong, "would never be so mad as to make an attempt on Washington, and it is therefore

Commodore Joshua Barney, already a naval hero, helped to save the capital city in 1814. (*U.S. Naval Institute, Annapolis, Md.*)

totally unnecessary to make any preparations for its defence."

The big battles of the war were still far to the north and west. The Indian leader Tecumseh was dead, and Andrew Jackson had quashed the Creek Nation. The remaining Native Americans had signed a treaty, and Americans who lived in the eastern cities imagined there no longer would be problems with them.

But the British raiding parties still traveled up the rivers that flowed into Chesapeake Bay. Almost every newspaper carried stories of their latest misdeeds along the waterfront. The villagers were learning how to cope with the nuisance. When a British ship appeared offshore, the townspeople hid what they could and warned everyone not to fire at the enemy in case anyone in town had a gun. Usually a raiding party burned down only what they thought was government property, stole some animals for food, and returned to their ships. They had been ordered not to destroy a private citizen's property. But if there was resistance of any kind, the raiders destroyed private property as well.

Near the end of June, scouts saw a large fleet of British ships and barges near the entrance to the Potomac River. But the British had found an easier route to the capital city. The ships sailed a little farther up the bay and went up the Patuxent River instead. British marines landed on shore and burned villages, then rowed back to their barges.

An "express" rode to Washington City to report the incident to Secretary of War Armstrong. He ordered soldiers to march south when another "express" arrived with the message that the barges had moved back down the river. Armstrong cancelled the orders. Two days later, a dozen barges struck again, farther up the river. Again and again they struck, only to disappear during the night.

Commodore Barney, whose flotilla of small ships was supposed to defend the Patuxent, found himself boxed in the river by the larger British ships. Barney set a few empty barges on fire and floated them down toward the British ships. But the best the Americans could do was set fire to the sails of one ship with "hot shot."

All of July the British ships sailed up and down the Patuxent, burned a few houses, stole supplies, and disappeared again. Much of the action was around the small town of Benedict, only thirty miles from Washington City. Winder's men captured six British soldiers and took them to Washington by coach, but they learned little from them. Meanwhile, many more civilians packed up their families and moved out of Washington City as fast as possible.

Admiral Cockburn's pirate crew was in the Potomac River, using the same attack-and-disappear tactics. They destroyed homes, looted, and then moved downstream before they could meet up with any angry militiamen. The plantation owners along the river worried not only about the British, but about rumors that the enemy might arm the slaves to rise up against them.

"The enemy's vessels have, for the present, nearly all left our river," said Winder confidently. He then concentrated on calling for all the militia to march to Bladensburg, Maryland, a town within a few miles of the capital. But Winder did not know the waterfront as well as the people who lived on it. They sent letters to the newspaper editor. "You give it as your opinion that enemy ships have left the Potomac," said one letter writer. "The fact is otherwise . . . the whole force is now just below the mouth of the St. Mary's River. The militia in this country . . . have so long been accustomed to the sight of the enemy that they are not afraid of them."

The British knew how poor communication was along Chesapeake Bay and took advantage of it. One American lookout would send off an express rider to report "a large fleet anchored off Drum Point." But another American lookout, watching the same activity from a different post on the river, would send the report, "There are only a few small vessels. It is because they move around so much that we think there are more of them."

Meanwhile in Washington City, usually deserted in August, the people threw open their doors to welcome the hero of the Battle of Lake Erie. Commodore Oliver Hazard Perry had put a large dent in the British plans to win back some of the land lost in the Revolution. Morale was low right then in the capital city, and people needed to celebrate Perry's success.

The Washington Theater company had reached the end of its season, but the actors put on a comedy followed by "a new Grand National Scene, being a spirited representation of the Battle and Victory on Lake Erie by our gallant Commodore Perry." The scene had been painted by a marine artist, Mr. Grain, and animated with behind-the-scene flashes of light and booming cannon noises. The audience had no idea how soon they would be hearing the real thing.

Suddenly on Wednesday, 17 August, the British ships all came together. They were joined by thirty more ships. Fifty-six sails, including six that were transport ships, probably carrying soldiers, horses, and cannons, moved up Chesapeake Bay. With the fleet were two line-of-battle ships, one flying the pennant of Admiral Cockburn, and the other, the pennant of Admiral Sir Alexander Cochrane. As the ships turned into the Patuxent River and headed toward the town of Benedict, lookouts sent off their express riders to Washington City.

On Thursday, the British officers unloaded their ships and had plenty of time to prepare their troops for the march ahead in a professional manner. No one resisted them because no one had stayed around Benedict after the raiding parties had begun shelling the town. The British spies in the capital city had been doing their job as well. They told their commanders that the British need not expect much resistance when they reached the end of their march.

General Winder was appalled. The enemy was not coming from the Potomac River, but from the other river? And how many were they? The best answer he could get was somewhere between four and sixteen thousand men. When he had last counted his own men, he had less than two thousand. With luck, he might get three thousand more. He was still not convinced, however, that the British were heading for Washington. Annapolis was a more likely target—and he had a dozen good reasons for believing they would march to Annapolis instead. Secretary of War Armstrong said he knew the British were most certainly going to Baltimore.

While their generals argued, the people of Washington City decided the time had come to save themselves. Rising dust clouds marked all the roads out of the city as men, women, and children grabbed anything with wheels to cart their families and valuables to a safe place. As each hot day passed and no one knew how close the enemy was, more Washingtonians left town. Government wagons, which should have been carrying food to the soldiers near Bladensburg, were all commandeered to carry important state papers, including the Declaration of Independence, to a place of hiding.

Dolley Madison calmly watched the exodus down Pennsylvania Avenue from her windows, but she found it hard to forget the threat made by the cocky Admiral Cockburn that he would be in her drawing room. The president held cabinet meetings at his house, but those meetings did not reassure her that all was under control.

James Monroe, who had fought under George Washington, was not about to sit around doing nothing, even though he was now secretary of state. He took a small escort and rode to Benedict himself to see what the enemy was doing.

At last, General Winder sent his couriers to call out the militia from all the states that had promised him help. Again many soldiers refused to step across their own state lines. The Pennsylvania militia sent word they could have come before their militia law expired in July, but now they could not make it before October. Many of the Maryland militia refused to march. The District Militia showed up at the base of Capitol Hill, most of them without guns, uniforms, or any other military equipment. Winder sent them home to arm themselves. "Even if you have to get kitchen knives! Then report to the Battalion Fields near Bladensburg."

Meanwhile, the British marched slowly and cautiously up the road that led to the city. Every second they expected to fall into a trap. The officers could hardly believe their eyes! No one had even felled trees over the road to slow their advance. No Americans attacked the rear. No flying parties hit their flanks and disappeared into the forest.

The August heat was unbearable. Never was such heat felt back in the British Isles. Many keeled over from heat exhaustion. The British were not intending to go to the capital city at all. They simply wanted to approach Commodore Barney's flotilla of small ships by a land route and destroy them. But this open road—all the way to the capital city—was too tempting for them to resist.

As for destroying Barney's flotilla, the secretary of the navy, William Jones, saved the British that trouble. He had ordered Barney to sink his own ships as soon as the British came too close. Barney unhappily obeyed his superior's orders to keep the British from seizing his ships. Then Barney and his men started a long, fast march across the peninsula to reach the city before the British did.

At noon on Sunday, the mayor of Washington ordered every able-bodied citizen and all free men of color to report to the Capitol at six the next morning and be ready to go to Bladensburg to build a large breastworks for the army to fight behind.

"Those who cannot attend in person," said the mayor, "will please send substitutes. Shovels, spades, and pickaxes will be furnished on the spot. Each man must take his provisions [food] for the day with him."

About five hundred men, white and black, showed up at daybreak Monday. "It is with much pleasure also we state," said the newspaper on Wednesday morning, "that on this occasion the free people of color in this city acted as became patriots. There is scarcely an exception of any failing to be on the spot and manifesting by their exertions all the zeal of freemen. At the same time, highly to their credit, conducting themselves with the utmost order and propriety."

On Monday, the president rode out with Armstrong and Jones, (the secretaries of the army and navy), and with Attorney General Richard Rush, to keep up the morale of the troops who were camped near Woodyard. They were not the only visitors. Most of the men and even many women who had remained in Washington City had also come out for the good sport of watching the soldiers fight the British. The eager spectators found comfortable places where they might have a good view and opened up their picnic baskets. When Madison left the camp the next afternoon, his group came within three miles of meeting the enemy head-on.

On Tuesday night, a scouting party told General Winder they had met the British advance guard not far from Woodyard. Winder broke all records making a retreat back into the city by 9:00 P.M., burning behind him the old bridge that crossed the eastern branch of the Potomac. He had sent most of his soldiers to guard the bridge at Bladensburg, but forgot to mention that it too should be blown up in case they had to retreat. He turned up at the President's House to explain that he had made a strategic move, so that his men would not be flattened by the British army during the night. The president sent him back, and Winder camped with his men on a hill above the new bridge over the eastern branch Tuesday night. This time he made arrangements to blow up the bridge if the enemy came on too strong.

By late Tuesday night there was no longer much doubt—even in General Winder's mind—where the British were heading. Three companies of cavalry had ridden down the road to see where the enemy was. Each company harassed the columns of redcoats from a different angle. They had exchanged shots and then turned their horses about in a hurry—but not before they had seen that the approaching army was very large and very well trained.

At the same time Colonel James Monroe, the secretary of state, was watching the enemy from what he hoped was a safe distance. He wrote a quick note and sent it off by express rider. President Madison received it about midnight on Tuesday. "The enemy are in full march for Washington. Have the materials prepared to destroy the bridges. You had better remove the records."

The reported size of the army shook up Winder. On Tuesday night he counted his own men again. Over two thousand men, commanded by General Joseph Stansbury, had just arrived, fortunately equipped with their own weapons. Another seven hundred men arrived from Virginia that day. In addition, General Walter Smith had brought over one thousand men from Georgetown, and that included the Federal City regiments. He could only hope that they were now armed with something better than kitchen knives.

Eleven hundred Marylanders had shown up. Commodore Barney had added his five hundred and twenty sailors and marines, and Lieutenant Colonel William Scott had three hundred regulars. No matter how Winder counted, the bad news was that in all his six thousand men, only nine hundred were trained soldiers. Coming toward him were almost five thousand soldiers—every one of them a veteran—and led by a professional soldier!

This professional, General Ross, led his men on first one road, and then another. At each turn, the American scouts sent off express riders with messages that the British were headed toward Washington—then it appeared they were headed more toward Annapolis. The messages arriving at General Winder's base were as confused as the scouts had been.

On Wednesday morning, General Ross's troops came to the very last branch on the road. Now at last, the express rider could go off with a correct message. Ross marched his men down the left fork. It was the road that led to the bridge over the eastern branch of the Potomac and into the capital city.

Ross stared straight ahead. He knew he was being watched. As soon as his own scouts told him that express riders had been seen galloping off toward Washington City, he ordered his troops to wheel about and face the opposite direction. His last column then had just passed the fork in the road. The last column then became the front line, and the British marched straight up the road toward Bladensburg.

12

The City Almost Dies

"I do not suppose the Government will ever return to Washington."

—Margaret Bayard Smith, August 1814

On Wednesday morning, 24 August, Washington's newspaper readers turned quickly to the editorial column on the daily paper's second page. And breathed sighs of relief. "Nearly the whole of yesterday passed off without any information of importance from our troops or those of the enemy," said the editorial, "except a report, for some time believed to be true, that the enemy had retrograded towards Nottingham."

The present editors, Gales and Seaton, added another relaxing note. "We feel assured that the number and bravery of our men will afford complete protection to the city."

At ten o'clock in the morning the city was deathly silent. Mrs. Thornton said that almost everyone she knew had left the city. Their own horses had been harnessed and ready to take off at a minute's notice since the day before. Dolley Madison was finishing a letter to her sister that she had begun the day before. She had just received a scribbled note from her husband, at the battlefield, to be ready to jump into her carriage and flee at a moment's warning. But she continued to write. "I have pressed as many Cabinet papers into trunks as to fill one carriage; our private property must be sacrificed as it is impossible to procure wagons for its transportation."

All offices and businesses were closed. Everything that was movable had been taken away. The townspeople had been warned not to shoot if the British came. Chances were the enemy would not destroy private property. Government property was their main objective.

James Madison had ridden off to the battlefield himself to see what was going on. About two thousand soldiers, under General Stansbury, had been left to guard the bridge at Bladensburg. Helping him were the Maryland militia and the exhausted sailors and marines of Commodore Joshua Barney. The heat was so intense that some soldiers on both sides died before any guns fired.

Only one other bridge had to be held in order to keep the British out of Washington. President Madison ordered General Winder, who had now moved to a safe retreat at the Navy Yard, to make a stand on the other side of the eastern branch of the Potomac in case the enemy should try to enter the city by the remaining bridge south of the Navy Yard. Winder's men finally got on their way about noon.

Armstrong was still flitting about the city, doing nothing. Madison ordered him to go with Winder and take the rest of the militia from the city. He obeyed, taking along with him Colonel Carroll and the hundred troops stationed at the President's House. This left Dolley Madison with only "French John" Sioussat, their steward, her harnessed carriage, and the Tunisia saber for protection.

At 1:00 P.M. the two armies clashed. Until that moment of impact at Bladensburg, most people still thought the British were marching to Annapolis or Baltimore. Madison sent an express messenger back to tell Dolley to leave.

"Will you believe it, my sister?" she was still writing in her letter at three o'clock. "We have had a battle, or skirmish, near Bladensburg, and here I am still within sound of the cannon! Mr. Madison comes not . . . but here I mean to wait for him."

Dolley had located another wagon and filled it with the most valuable articles that belonged to the President's House. Madison finally sent Colonel Charles Carroll to force Dolley to leave at once.

"Our kind friend Mr. Carroll has come to hasten my departure, and in a very bad humor with me because I insist on waiting until the large picture of General Washington [the painting by Gilbert Stuart] is secured, and it requires to be unscrewed from the wall." Finally the frame was broken. The canvas painting was rolled up and entrusted to two gentlemen from New York, Jacob Barker and Robert G. L. de Peyster. Dolley scribbled a final sentence to her sister's letter and left with her maid, Sukey.

Near Bladensburg, a scout topped a hill suddenly to discover President Madison and Secretary of State Monroe. They were within range of the British guns, the surprised scout shouted at them. The British were approaching just over the hill. Rockets began screaming down on their position. Only then did they realize what a coup it would be for the British to take prisoner some of the nation's top leaders. They raced toward the city. So did a crowd of sightseers who had come out to watch the battle and suddenly decided they had seen enough.

In less than an hour it was over. The British general

Ross led his men across the Bladensburg bridge to the Washington City side. The Americans dropped everything and fled. Even so, the militiamen did not reach the city before their fearless leaders, Winder and Armstrong. This shameful retreat was later called "The Bladensburg Races."

Winder tried to make a report later of what happened, but it was obvious that he had not stayed around very long. He and all the defeated troops following him fled north to the town of Montgomery Court House. He claimed the British had four hundred killed, while he guessed that the Americans had maybe lost thirty or forty. A later count showed that thirty men had been killed in Commodore Barney's company alone.

Commodore Barney had arrived at Bladensburg on Tuesday, after sinking his own barges in the Patuxent. He then had been ordered by Winder to withdraw with his men to the bridge near the Navy Yard. Barney's men were ordered to defend that bridge, or blow it up if the British came too close. The secretary of the navy, meanwhile, came by and ordered Barney to march his men back again to Bladensburg. Barney, riding far ahead, discovered they were just in time for the battle. He sent an officer racing back to have his men "come up in a trot." The exhausted men arrived just as the battle began. Barney's men took their position on rising ground and fired as the enemy came up the road toward them. "By this time," said Barney, "not a vestige of the American army remained except a body of five or six hundred posted on a height on my right."

Barney's horse was shot from under him. Then his men were surrounded, and the Americans above him gave up. Barney was wounded badly in the thigh and ordered his men to leave him behind. Huffington, an officer, stayed with him. A British officer came up to them and, realizing Barney's importance, had the two men taken to General Ross and Admiral Cockburn.

War was polite in 1814 when enemies had to deal with each other face to face. Brave officers, like Barney and Huffington, were treated by the enemy with the same respect and care they would have given a brother officer. A surgeon treated Barney's leg wound, although he did not remove the ball from it, and Barney was carried on a litter to Bladensburg. The next day he was released "on parole," because it was obvious he would not be fighting again very soon. Both sides agreed to exchange prisoners and Barney was back in action before long.

Back on the battlefield, doctors treated both American and British soldiers. At least a dozen had died from the heat, without a sign of a wound, but there was no time for burying the dead until the wounded had been cared for.

At twilight on Wednesday, the British marched down Maryland Avenue into the silent city. A young British officer, whose diary is today in the archives of the U.S. Naval Academy at Annapolis, tells his side of "The Entrance into Washington":

"In the evening when the army advanced upon Washington, General Ross halted it outside the town and sent in a flag of truce to treat of its surrender. No person could be found to receive it, but the General ordered it in again, and at the same time followed it himself, when, as he was passing the first house of the town, a volley of musketry was fired at him and he had again his horse shot under him, and several of the people about him killed and wounded. [The general's piebald horse had been killed that afternoon at Bladensburg.] The house was immediately stormed, but the fellows who had been in it had time to escape by the back court [yard]. This house was immediately set on fire and it,

The British army in Washington, D.C. This picture was published in a book for British schoolchildren. (*Library of Congress*)

with another which caught fire by accident from the flames of the Capitol, was the only private property injured by the English army during the time Washington remained in its possession."

At the Capitol building the British fired into the windows, then broke the locks on the doors and poured inside. Kegs of gunpowder and rockets, heaped up with books, papers, and broken furniture exploded into blazes so hot that some of the marble pillars cracked. The wooden porch connecting the two houses went first. Then the wooden floors burned through. In an upper floor of the Senate wing, the valuable Library of Congress went up in flames. An hour later, only the blackened walls were left.

Excited by the scene at the Capitol the British, led by both Ross and Cockburn, hurried on down Pennsylvania Avenue to the President's House and the Treasury. Cockburn

This engraving was published in England the following October. In small print under the picture: "On August 24, 1814 when we burnt and destroyed their Dock Yard with a Frigate and a Sloop of War, Rope-walk, Arsenal, Senate House, President's Palace, War Office, Treasury, and the Great Bridge. With the Flotilla the public property destroyed amounted to thirty Million of Dollars."

At top right is (A) General Ross and the British army with (B) cannon taken from the Americans. At (C) is the city of Washington; (D) the American Flotilla destroyed; (E) the Dock Yard and Arsenal burnt; (F) the Rope-walk; (G) the River Potowmack; (H) the Great Bridge destroyed; (I) the War Office; (K) the President's Palace on fire; (L) the Senate House; (M) the Treasury. (*Library of Congress*)

took particular pleasure in making good his threat to stand in Dolley Madison's drawing room. In short time the soldiers had helped themselves to the food and wine, to Dolley's personal clothing, and to all other valuables that they could carry away. They broke up the furniture, tore down the draperies, and threw Madison's books into the center of the rooms. By midnight all the windows were ablaze and the flames licking up the white outside walls.

From across the Potomac River most of the escaped citizens watched the enemy fires burn down their city. The damage actually looked a great deal worse than it turned out to be. The new Potomac Bridge to Alexandria had been destroyed at one end so the British could not cross.

The British were too slow arriving at the Navy Yard to do much damage there. Commandant Thomas Tingey had blown up and burned everything he did not want the British to get, including some new ships. So little was left for Ross's men that the British had to content themselves with spiking every cannon they found by pounding a spike into the touchhole of each one so it could not be fired. Before they left the powder magazine at Greenleaf Point, the Americans spiked the guns they left behind. They had also hidden many barrels of powder in a dry well. After the British blew up the powder magazine, a few of their soldiers casually dropped some matches in the well. "The effect was terrific," said the newspaper later. "Every soldier was blown into eternity, and many at a greater distance were wounded."

The British officer's diary tells the story of the powder magazine a little differently. He said, "The powder magazines were of course set on fire and exploded with a tremendous crash, throwing down many houses in their vicinity, partly by pieces of the walls striking them and partly by the concussion of the air; whilst quantities of shot, shell, and hand grenades which could not be otherwise rendered useless, were thrown into the river."

The heat of the day still hung around at midnight, and with the heat and smoke from the fires added to it the night was almost unbearable. The soldiers retired to a temporary camp near the Capitol and fell into exhausted sleep. Ross and Cockburn, meanwhile, went to a tavern near the Treasury building and demanded that a frightened landlady give them supper.

"The lady of the house where the British officers supped on the evening they entered the city," reported the newspaper several days after the event, "recognized among them a person who had been at her house and had even called on Mrs. Madison in the President's House in the disguise of a distressed woman on the Saturday preceding the capture of the city."

The next morning was gray and hot. Heavy humidity held the smoky smell from the last night's destruction, and the enemy troops had little of the previous night's pep. Dr. Thornton and his wife had stayed with friends in Georgetown because the roads outside town had been too crowded with fleeing American militia. At breakfast, Dr. Thornton heard that the British were getting ready to burn the War Office, as well as the public building that held his patent office. He hurried with Colonel Carroll into the city to save his patent models.

They arrived just as the War Office was put to the torch. Both men pleaded with Colonel Jones, the British officer in charge. "This is not a government building," Thornton begged. "It is a Museum of the Arts and would be a loss to all the world . . . some are musical instruments."

"You may take out any private property in the building," the colonel suggested.

"Nothing but private property is in that building," insisted Thornton. "To burn what would be useful to all mankind would be as barbarous as when the Turks burned down the Alexandria Library [one of the famous Seven Wonders of the Ancient World]!"

The colonel withdrew his men, and the Patent Office was saved.

The editor of the *National Intelligencer* did not fare as well. Cockburn, especially, had been enraged by the editorials written about him in the newspaper. And unluckily for Gales and Seaton, Cockburn was in charge. He turned a deaf ear to the owners' pleas that he was destroying private property. Cockburn did not believe the owners when they insisted that newspapers in the United States were not run by the government.

Storming and raging, Cockburn ordered his men to completely destroy all of the type, the machines, and the paper supply. "And be sure that all the C's are destroyed," he is reported to have shouted after his men, "so that the rascals can have no further means of abusing me as they have done."

About seven o'clock, a dead calm and the tropical heat slowed down the enemy again. Then suddenly Nature struck a blow. A roaring wind descended, with monsoon rains that quickly put out any remaining flames. Roofs blew off houses in the town and flew through the air like sheets of paper, according to a British writer. Sections of chimneys and fences sailed down streets, as destructive as cannon balls. Trees were "twisted off their roots." Some houses blew down, and thirty British soldiers were crushed inside. Their camp was almost completely blown away. "Two cannons standing upon a bit of rising ground were fairly lifted up into the air and carried several yards to the rear," reported the British, who had seen such a "hurricane" only on the seas.

By nine o'clock on Thursday night the storm ended. The British leaders were now anxious to get their men back to the ships. They had heard rumors of ten thousand angry Americans heading their way. And standing ankle-deep in mud, they could do no more harm to the city. They went back the way they had come—across the Bladensburg battlefield where many of their dead and wounded still lay.

On Friday, 26 August, the townspeople began coming

back. And not a moment too soon. Vandals had run free in the city after the British left. Looters had helped themselves to valuable government property.

Gales and Seaton managed to buy a small amount of type, and a Baltimore newspaper loaned them a machine. Four days after the British left, they were back in business with a one-page newspaper. "No houses were half as much plundered by the enemy as by the knavish wretches about the town who profited of the general distress," reported the *National Intelligencer*.

13

Rebirth

"What! Desert the Capitol? Let Congress rather cover it with canvass and sit in its ruins, than abandon it at this moment!"

—Anonymous military officer, 30 August 1814

The newspaper squelched for the last time the idea of moving the seat of government. The people of Washington City had bought property, built public offices, and now had even suffered together an invasion by the enemy. Philadelphia's invitation to move the government back to Pennsylvania went unanswered.

The most urgent business was burying the dead, British as well as Americans. Many still lay out near Bladensburg where a citizen's committee rode out to dig graves.

The wounded were carried into the city. Dr. Catlett set up a general hospital on Capitol Hill for all the sick and wounded regulars and militia. Dr. James Ewell took care of the British wounded, although there was little money to pay for their care.

The building that held Dr. Thornton's patent office, as

The President's House, after its destruction by the British on Wednesday, 24 August 1814 (*Library of Congress*)

well as the General Post Office, had once been known as Blodget's Hotel. It was now the largest building left undamaged in the city, and Congress moved into it at once.

The president and Mrs. Madison had lost all of their personal possessions during the one-day invasion. They spent some nights with the Cutts family (Mrs. Cutts was Dolley's sister), and then moved into Mr. Tayloe's Octagon House, where the French minister had been living.

Judge Duvall gave his house for the Department of State. The house where the British minister had lived now became the Treasury Department. The War Office moved into a building next to the Bank of the Metropolis. Mr. Way offered one of his new houses for the Post Office.

While Congress sat in what was once Blodget's Hotel, the citizens of Washington formed the "Capitol Hotel Company" to raise money to build a temporary home for Con-

The Capitol in ruins after the fire. The wooden arcade joining the two buildings was completely burned. (*The National Archives*)

gress. Although many congressmen still spoke of moving the seat of government, the whole community rallied so strongly to rebuild the city that their spirit prevailed. Congress voted to restore the old burned-out Capitol. They were to meet in the temporary "Old Brick Capitol" for the next four years, a building that lasted—with some remodeling—until 1932.

The Library of Congress, stored in the Senate building, was gone. But Thomas Jefferson wrote in September to offer his own collection of books. For fifty years, Jefferson had been collecting rare books on America. The collection he sold to Congress filled twenty wagons.

Secretary of War John Armstrong resigned. James Monroe, who had really been doing all of the military jobs anyway, now became secretary of war, and commander in chief of the military district (Winder's job), as well as being secretary of state. Dr. James H. Blake, mayor of the city, was much criticized for running away in time of danger. Everyone agreed the militia was cowardly.

The British sailed up the Potomac River on the following Saturday and threw the city into another panic. Only Fort Warburton, down the Potomac, stood between the capital and another visit from the British ships. And then the fort was gone. The American captain in charge of Fort Warburton blew it up without firing a shot, no doubt startling the British as much as Washingtonians. He claimed General Winder had told him to do it and escape across the river, rather than surrender it. As a result, the British sailed freely up the Potomac, and entered Alexandria, robbing its citizens of everything that looked valuable. But they did not enter Washington City again.

If nothing else came of the burning of Washington, at least the bold deed by the British had succeeded in uniting the Americans to defend their country. A Richmond, Virginia, newspaper reported that the capital city was totally destroyed and called out their own volunteers. New York, Baltimore, and Philadelphia newspapers rounded up all their own militia. The people of Baltimore, especially worried they would be next, prepared for war.

But Washington City was still very much alive. President Madison called a special session of Congress on 19 September. They all managed to crowd into the old Blodget's Hotel building, although the House of Representatives' members were squashed in up to the fireplace. Shop owners brought out the goods they had hidden and opened for business. The ladies began their tea parties and citizens called on one another to ask, "Where were you when the British came, and what did you do?"

The British soldiers struggled down muddy roads back to their ships at the town of Benedict, taking their wounded with them and only a few prisoners. Dr. William Beanes of Marlborough was one of the unlucky few. He had been captured only the week before when a British officer caught him outside after curfew. Even though the doctor argued that he was only caring for his patients, the British held him for a few days before releasing him on parole. Now, as the

British soldiers hastened back to their ships, an informer told some of the officers that the same Dr. Beanes had violated his parole once more. The informant had seen the doctor caring for some straggling Americans after the fighting. The angry officers beat on Dr. Beanes's door in the middle of the night, hardly allowing him time to dress properly, and took him on board one of the ships as a prisoner.

A few weeks later the ship, with Dr. William Beanes still a prisoner, was anchored in the Patapsco River off Baltimore. Two of Beanes's friends from Washington, Francis Scott Key and John S. Skinner, went to the secretary of state, James Monroe, to ask his permission to try to have the doctor released. But by the time they climbed aboard the ship where the prisoner was being held, they could see signs that the British were planning to attack Baltimore harbor.

Although the British agreed to release their friend, they insisted that all three remain on board a ship to the rear of the action until the battle ended. All the night of 13 September 1814 the anxious three paced the deck watching the fierce bombardment of Fort McHenry at the entrance to the harbor. An immense flag—each star measured two feet across—flew over the fort, but in the dark of night the men could see it only when a Congreve rocket lit up the sky momentarily. By daybreak the smoke and haze hid the fort completely. Had the American flag been lowered to be replaced by the British flag? The answer came suddenly when the fog lifted gradually—and the sight he saw so inspired Francis Scott Key that he immediately began jotting down words that became a poem on the back of an envelope.

In the 16 January 1815 Washington newspaper was an advertisement. "A favorite patriotic song" named "The Star-Spangled Banner" was now offered for sale at the music store in Georgetown.

Where the Information Came From

Tidbits of the city's daily life, the shops, new bridges, police reports, Samuel Harrison Smith's battle for freedom of the press, parades, the U.S. Navy ships in 1809, invasion by the British, and many other portions of the book came from articles and advertisements found in these newspapers:

> The *Washington City Gazette*, 1796–1800
> The *Washington Federalist*, 1800
> The *Times and District of Columbia Daily Advertiser*, 1801
> The *National Intelligencer*, 1801–1815

Descriptions of the city as it was planned, its advantages over other cities, its river, and how it looked in the earliest days, are from such books as:

> S. S. Moore and T. W. Jones's *Traveller's Directory*, 1804
> Tobias Lear's *Observations on the River Potowmack, the Country Adjacent, and the City of Washington*, 1793

Eyewitness descriptions of the city, its people, and its happenings are from diaries and letters written by:

Adams, Abigail, 1800	Madison, Dolley, 1809–1814
Adams, John, 1800	Satterthwaite, Abel, 1813
Beebe, Lewis, 1800	Smith, Margaret Bayard, 1800–1814
Kent, James, 1793–1794	Thornton, Anna Maria, 1800–1814

Details and descriptions of the battle at Bladensburg, the burning of Washington City, and the capture of Dr. William Beanes, in 1814, came from accounts written by the following eyewitnesses:

Armstrong, John, secretary of war	Smith, Margaret Bayard
Barney, Commodore Joshua	Thornton, Anna Maria
Madison, Dolley	Thornton, Dr. William
Monroe, Colonel James	Tingey, Commandant Thomas
Rodgers, Commodore John	

Bibliography

Adams, Abigail. *Letters of Mrs. Adams*. Edited by Charles F. Adams. Boston: Little, Brown, 1840.

———. *New Letters of Abigail Adams*. Edited by Steward Mitchell. Boston: Houghton Mifflin, 1947.

Adams, John. *Diary and Autobiography*. Cambridge: Harvard University Press, 1961.

Bedini, Silvio A. "The Survey of the Federal Territory." *Washington History* 3 (Spring/Summer 1991): 76–95.

Clark, Allen Culling. *Life and Letters of Dolly Madison*. Washington, D.C.: Press of W. F. Roberts, 1914.

Compilation of the Messages and Papers of the Presidents 1789–1897. Edited by Jason D. Richardson. Vol. 1. Washington, D.C.: Government Printing Office, 1896.

Cope, Thomas P. *Philadelphia Merchant: Diary of Thomas P. Cope*. Edited by Eliza Cope Harrison. South Bend, Ind.: Gateway Editions, 1978.

Goode, James M. *Capital Losses: A Cultural History of Washington's Destroyed Buildings*. Washington, D.C.: Smithsonian Institution Press, 1979.

Green, Constance McL. *Washington: Village and Capital, 1800–1878*. Princeton, N.J.: Princeton University Press, 1962.

Hawkins, Don Alexander. "The Landscape of the Federal City." *Washington History* 3 (Spring/Summer 1991): 10–33.

Jefferson, Thomas. *Life and Selected Writings of Thomas Jefferson*. Edited by Adrienne Koch and William Peden. New York: Random House, Modern Library, 1944.

———. *The Papers of Thomas Jefferson*. Vol. 20. Edited by Julian Boyd. Princeton, N.J.: Princeton University Press, 1982.

Lear, Tobias. *Observations on the River Potowmack, the Country Adjacent, and the City of Washington*. New York, 1793.

Maclay, William. *Journal of William Maclay*. Edited by Edgar Maclay. New York: Appleton and Company, 1890.

Malone, Dumas. *Jefferson the President: First Term, 1801–1805*. Boston: Little, Brown, 1970.

———. *Jefferson the President: Second Term, 1805–1809*. Boston: Little, Brown, 1974.

Melder, Keith, ed. *City of Magnificent Intentions: A History of the District of Columbia*. Washington, D.C.: D.C. Public Schools, 1983.

Moore, S. S., and T. W. Jones. *The Traveller's Directory, or Pocket Companion*. 2d edition. Philadelphia, 1804.

"A New View of Blodget's Hotel." *Washington History* 2 (Spring 1990): 103–105.

Nimitz Library, U.S. Naval Academy, Annapolis, Md. Diary of unidentified British naval officer.

Scott, Pamela. "L'Enfant's Washington Described." *Washington History* 3 (Spring/Summer 1991): 96–111.

Seale, William. *The President's House: A History*. 2 vols. Wash-

ington, D.C.: White House Historical Association in coopera-
tion with the National Geographic Society, 1986.

Smith, Margaret Bayard. *The First Forty Years of Washington
Society in Family Letters of Margaret Bayard Smith.* Edited
by Hunt Gaillard. New York: Frederick Ungar, 1965.

————. "The President's House Forty Years Ago." *Godey's Lady's
Book,* November 1843, 212–213.

Smith, Page. *John Adams.* 2 vols. Garden City, N.Y.: Doubleday,
1962.

Thane, Elswyth. *Dolley Madison: Her Life and Times.* New
York: Crowell-Collier Press, 1970.

Thornton, Anna Maria. "Diary of Mrs. William Thornton." Columbia Historical Society Records 10: 88–226.

Washington, George. *Writings of George Washington, 1745–1799.*
Edited by John C. Fitzpatrick. Boston: Houghton Mifflin,
1925.

Wilson, Rufus Rockwell. *Washington, the Capital City.* Vol. 1.
Philadelphia: J. B. Lippincott, 1902.

Index

155